TOO **FAT**
TOO **LOUD**
TOO **AMBITIOUS**

A SEXY BRILLIANT HANDBOOK

devina kaur

Devina Care Group Inc.

ISBN 978-1-7771176-0-3

Interior design by VeeVee Creative Studio & Aaxel Author Services

To you, the warrior. May you be the wellspring of power and light in your pursuit of eternal love within and around you.

Table of Contents

Introduction

L ife is an orgasm! *Too Fat Too Loud Too Ambitious* will encourage you to embrace your Sexy Brilliance. You will learn how to be daring. You will scream your truth and put yourself out in the world in a powerful way. You will practice being unapologetically true to yourself and radically accepting who you are in your entirety. With this book, you will make your life, in its entirety, as pleasurable as an orgasm should be. Most importantly, you will learn to love yourself more and give yourself the courage to be yourself in order to live your most pleasurable life.

Too Fat Too Loud Too Ambitious is the first book in the Sexy Brilliant™ series. Writing this book was a labour of relentless optimism, and it is intended to bring love, happiness, and passion into your life. Throughout this book, possibly the world's first-ever X-rated self-help book, I can offer you support and guidance towards finding your authenticity and truthful living. My own story is a lesson in overcoming the odds to find happiness, peace, and pleasure. I am committed to helping you grow, by revealing real, raw, and relatable personal experiences that I have been through and survived. From an eating disorder to low self-esteem to manic depressive mood swings, I have gone through a lot to become the "Divine Devina." I hope that telling you the truth about myself will show you that you are not alone— you are *alive*. If you have ever felt unhappy within yourself and are searching for deeper meaning in life, please know this book is for you. This book is my gift to you. It will help you become a sexier version of yourself.

I am grateful to help you advance in your sexy journey toward being the brilliant star that you already are.

Too Fat Too Loud Too Ambitious is divided into two sections. In the first three chapters, I will share my journey from my strict, traditional upbringing in India, to my self-loving, fabulous life in Canada. The chapters will discuss how I transformed my mindset to turn these flaws into freedom through self-acceptance, awareness, and mindful living. Throughout, you will see how I lived up to my own Sexy Brilliance—and how you can, too. Each chapter is dedicated to a quality I was told that I was failing. However, as it turns out, being "*too fat*" or "*too loud*" or "*too ambitious*" is not a bad thing at all. In fact, a person can't be too much of anything; being who you are is empowering and gives you spiritual confidence. Knowing your inner power makes you truly unique.

Before taking care of others, you must take care of yourself. Whether you like it or not, you have to be connected to the Divine before you can work with and inspire others. *Too Fat Too Loud Too Ambitious* will guide you to explore your most intimate experiences, fantasies, and beliefs.

In the latter half of the book, some practical tools on self-awareness will be explored and provided in order to live a more self-fulfilling life. You may have a less-than-ecstatic response. The issues I address in this book may push you toward an emotional low. If you cry or get depressed, please remember that this is often the case when you are going through difficult transformation. Remind yourself that life is a journey. Breathe and be at zero.

Disclaimer: I do not pretend to be a therapist or a coach. Please seek professional help if you encounter issues, emotions, or life experiences that are too difficult to understand and process.

Throughout this book, you will find vocabulary, concepts,

challenges, and activities that will connect you to your own Sexy Brilliance. You might feel excited, uncomfortable, or just plain horny! At any time, you may have an intense physical response to what you read. For example, you may have the impulse to do yoga, naked. You may need an anal break! You may want to take your clothes off while you read, or put on your favourite music and dance. That is normal and healthy. You may also feel intense stress. If you do feel that way, it is okay to release your emotions through masturbation.

In short, this book will make you uncomfortable—in which case, do not hesitate to jerk off!

If you need a break, try some or all of the following sexy techniques to get deeper into your divine self and get the release your body craves.

Meditation Break

Meditation is always an opportunity to masturbate! Take some private time for yourself to connect with your innermost thoughts and desires. You can go deep within your own inner workings and find a place where your fantasies come to life. Sit on a soft pillow, touch yourself, play with yourself, say a healing mantra. Whether you choose to meditate or to masturbate, there is no "right" choice. Both meditation and masturbation are ways to get to know yourself better and better. Both of these activities can support that.

Gratitude Break

Adopting an attitude of gratitude for all things helps you let go of difficult events and situations when you need to, while attracting more of what you need. Being grateful for all things creates a loving atmosphere that serves as a type of filter for our energy field. If you are not sure where to begin, try visualizing the face of the person you love most. Maybe it's your own! You can write a love letter to yourself, or make a list of the people, things, and blessings you are most grateful for. These are loving intentions that connect you with the universe.

Yoga Break

Exercise, even doing yoga, can help you to get out of your head and into your body. When you spend too much time in your mind, you tend to over think. You might fall into thought patterns that do not serve your highest self, and therefore others. Spending time in a yoga pose or on a nature walk helps you slow down and focus on your breathing. Remember that in your breath, you are not alone. Be in the flow of life knowing there is no need to fret about things you cannot control.

Forgiveness Break

Forgiveness is not always an easy task. However, when you say, "I forgive you," the negative energy in your connection starts to melt away. There are activities in this book that will help you work through significant resentments, but those three little words have a lot of power. Say them to yourself. Say them to an empty room. Say them without moving your lips. You deserve to forgive—and to be forgiven.

Someone may have hurt you very deeply at one time, and as a part of your story, you hold on to this hurt because it impacted you so greatly. When it's a habit, or learned, repeated behaviour, staying in suffering is easier than forgiving. You deserve to let go of your pain and suffering. You can do this at any time by simply saying, "I forgive you."

I would also like to take this moment to ask you for

forgiveness should anything in this book or in the Sexy Brilliant™ work upset you. Thank you.

Banana Break

At any point in your process, you may need some fuel! Bananas are one of the healthiest fruits available. Eating healthy is so important. It will help you maintain your energy levels and your overall sense of well-being. To get the most out of the fuel you put into your body, eat holistically, organically, and follow universal laws when you can. When you eat organic bananas you also care more for the planet Earth, as organic harvest is better for our environment.

P.S. If you decide to put that banana anywhere but your mouth, put a condom on it!

Shower Break

Showers, bathing, and connecting with the flow of water is another beautiful way to cleanse your energy. The beauty is that you can do this every day. Showers keep you functioning at a high vibration, by rinsing away the energies you pick up on a daily basis. You'd be surprised by what you pick up just going about your daily life.

Ideally practised upon waking up and before going to bed, water-based meditation breaks bring peace and soothing to your ethereal body as well as to your physical self. Every time you take a shower, stand with your head in the water. Visualize a golden light passing through your head, your arms, and your legs. If you do not have access to a shower or running water, simply washing your feet, face, and hands while visualizing golden light around you is equally helpful.

Bring to your awareness any daily stress, anxiety, and energies that do not belong to you. In order to release them, imagine them flowing away from you, down the drain. Concentrate on the sensation of the water on your skin. Let the flow of the water wash away any lower-vibration thoughts as they arise: regret, guilt, sadness, anger, depression, temper, and anything else that does not serve you.

Let it all drain away, and feel your body become lighter. Enjoy this moment for what it is. Allow the water to bring clarity to your thoughts. Now, your soul can be free. You are renewed.

Anal Break

When masturbation and other kinds of sex are not giving you the relief you need, try something different. Anal sex will change your perspective, in more ways than one! If you think about it, life is an anal passage. Sometimes, it seems very hard to get in. Yet, once you understand the technique, it becomes very pleasurable. When you need a break after morning coffee or before dinner, try making it an anal break.

Be bold. Dare. Why go the easy way? Challenge your comfort zone. Be strategic; be unapologetic. And yes, it will get messy, but once you hit the pleasure point, it might be the biggest release of your life. Once you find your anal technique, you will be able to go through anything in life.

Finally, at any time, feel free to revisit these methods of release, relaxation, and self-love. I encourage you to open your heart and begin your transformation from a place of self-awareness. As of this moment, your path is not dictated by your wounds. You are not lacking. Your life is abundant with opportunities, not obstacles.

The Sexy Brilliant™ movement will connect you to your inner, divine self. And that is sexy!

You were born beautiful, and you have a light within you that brings out your own special brilliance. That light empowers you and helps you embrace your truest self. You are a unique, sexy being, and your being is a divine creation. You are a gift made by the Divine who has put you in this physical form to experience a beautiful life on planet Earth. You have the power to be the change and to be the brilliance that will pave the way for many people. You have the power to heal the lives you touch.

You can help heal the world by self-knowledge, self-acceptance, and healing yourself through love. *Too Fat Too Loud Too Ambitious* will guide you through the work of being more loving toward yourself. It is impossible to take care of others when you do not take care of yourself. When you practice self-care, you are able to help and heal others, as well as yourself.

With the help of many professionals, I have developed the K.A.U.R.™ Process, which is discussed in the second part of this book. This process will help you find the inner sexiness and brilliance that is already yours. It will help you find your way and understand your experience of what it means to be *Sexy Brilliant*.

I am so excited for you to start this journey! Let's begin

One million Sexy Brilliant, divine, kisses,
In love, gratitude, and mutual respect,
Namaste,

Devina Kaur™

Chapter Zero

This is Chapter Zero: the beginning before the beginning.

Zero is the unknown, and it represents the fearless. Zero is zen. Today, right now, this moment is yours because every moment matters. May this be your Chapter Zero too; may it be a new beginning, a new day, a new era.

My intention for this book is symbolized by the wholeness, fullness, and roundness of zero. Zero is a symbol of completion. It is the origin, it represents the place you come from. It represents *now*-ness. The moment you are in is where you will find your bliss.

So often, people look for fulfilment outside of the moment. If you do, you are fooling yourself. *This* is the only moment that matters. I too, used to look for a high from the next moment. Living in the moment was never enough for me. I was always searching for my next snack, my next lover, or my next adventure. However, when I discovered my life purpose of *Sexy Brilliant*, it became everything I have been searching for.

What Is Sexy Brilliant?

First of all, I want to be honest and upfront with you, Sexy Brilliant happened accidentally. I created the Sexy Brilliant™ Global Revolution while overcoming my addiction. I will share more details on this later on in the book.

Secondly, Sexy Brilliant™ is the ideal at the core of *Too Fat Too Loud Too Ambitious*. To me, Sexy Brilliance and success are synonymous. Sexy Brilliance is a way of being that is available to anyone. It is a lifestyle. It is a mindset that you can choose at any moment. It encompasses the physical, emotional, spiritual, and intellectual domains.

Although Sexy Brilliance can unlock unbelievable success and wealth, it is so much more than riches, blessings, and money. Sexy Brilliant people are daring, confident, outspoken, and loving. They experience and demonstrate acceptance of their added confidence, body image, and individual worth, no matter their age. Sexy Brilliance is a sense of grace, elegance, and authenticity that empowers people to recognize their own strength, beauty, gifts, and inner light.

Sexy Brilliant people are genuine, they live unapologetically, and they do not have to follow because they *lead* with their own instincts. They do what they know is right for them. For example, I sit on the floor to eat when I can. It keeps me grounded. Sitting and eating on the ground is an ancient custom, and was practised by many of our ancestors, and even today it helps us stay connected to the natural energy of the Earth.

One of the biggest criticisms that I hear about Sexy Brilliant is that it is egotistical, even though it is actually a not-for-profit movement and a foundation. In the act of celebrating myself, I am labelled as self-centred or self-absorbed. Some people say I lack humility. Nothing could be further from the truth. Sexy Brilliant™ as a philosophy brings balance between myself and my stress and puts *me* at the centre of *my* life. I have come to realize that there is nothing wrong with that. You are allowed to be the star of your own movie!

It is not egotistical to love yourself. There is a pervasive belief that the ego is the 'bad guy' of the psyche. The ego keeps you alive. It allows you to assert your needs for food, sleep, safety, security, sex, and money. The ego provides the instinct for self-preservation that is required to survive.

Instead of vilifying it, make friends with your ego through self-acceptance, self-work, and self-love. Doing this inner work might require you to challenge your cultural heritage. You may have to face your fears around the concept of change as you connect to inner divinity. The hardest thing in the beginning is learning to listen to your spiritual, inner voice.

Yet, who are you living for? Whose life is this, anyway? Yours.

How Do I Use This Book?

To begin your own transformation, plan to set aside at least one hour a day, for thirty consecutive days. This is the time you will need to practice the strategies I offer in *Too Fat Too Loud Too Ambitious*. You will find many tools in this book. The introduction includes a few "breaks" that will help you to grow, release, and unwind. I would suggest that you try some if not all of them. Take the time to get acquainted with each one. The investment of your time is all it is going to take toward achieving a Sexy Brilliant life.

You may believe that you do not have that much time. Of course, it sounds like a lot! But consider this: while you may be busy, time does not really exist in the spiritual world. Neither do excuses. You do not grow unless you commit to the process. So, as of this moment, you must make *yourself* your number one priority.

Be stronger than your excuses. Be determined to be Sexy Brilliant.

What Is Sexy?

Sexiness is defined by how a person lives and the energy they project. You are a divine spiritual being, and you are meant to live a life full of fun, laughter, and happiness. You become sexy through the expression of your feelings.

Many people say that sex appeal is about appearance. Usually what one first notices about others is their physical traits, but sexiness is a feeling that starts from the inside.

Being sexy also includes how you treat and support others. Sexy Brilliant people are always interested in other people. They are always working to empower others. They always help others achieve their dreams and goals without any expectations, while simultaneously focusing on themselves and their own personal growth.

It is correct to assume that sexy people give without hoping for or expecting anything in return. My favourite poet, William Wordsworth said, *"The best part of a good man's life is his little nameless unremembered acts of kindness and love."* You should release your expectations of others because you do not need them! You must know and have faith that when you need help, it will be there. Sexy people attract others like them, who are equally successful, equally important, and equally sexy. Although you never attach a price tag to the love you give, you should always remember the people who helped you on your journey. Give thanks to them for the lessons that they taught you.

Everyone that you allow into your life can teach you something new. You should remember to practice constant gratitude and to keep your heart and mind open for unique and alternative ways that you can help empower others and make a difference in the world. The flow of love, compassion, success, and care between people is the deepest, sexiest connection imaginable.

What Is the Sexy Divine?

Sexy, divine people are those who are open. I mean really, truly open. When you tap into your sexy divine self, you begin the process of getting to know, accept, and love yourself and others at all levels. Sexy Divine includes the mind, body, soul, and spirit. In the sexy divine, we celebrate our so-called "imperfections." You are in tune with your sexiness, and you focus on personal growth, self-awareness, and self-regulation. Although others may not value them, these qualities are immensely powerful to us.

A few words about "imperfections," which I prefer to call "perfections." If someone tells you that you are imperfect, it creates an inadequacy or doubt in your mind. When you think positively, you change your focus. Acknowledging your "imperfections" as blessings changes your perspective so you can experience life based on your own truth and sexy divinity.

If you remove the idea of "imperfections" from your heart and mind, you will be drawn more towards Sexy Brilliance. Nothing stops you from being naturally in touch with your divine, spiritual, inner wisdom. All you need to do is to start embracing the idea that you are sexy just the way you are! In my experience I can assure you that the only thing stopping you from being empowered is yourself, and you can change that, any time you want.

You do not love others simply because they are "perfect." You love them just the way they are in their wholeness. Are you able to do the same for yourself? Let us love ourselves with the same intensity. If you are struggling with self-acceptance, here is your mantra to repeat: *I am perfect as I am!* The more you say it to yourself the more you will find yourself believing in it.

You are perfect as you are. The minute you start accepting yourself and stop thinking of yourself as inadequate, you become irresistible to the world. Self-acceptance is the key to celebrating the sexiness that resides inside all of us.

Why Is Solitude Important?

Part of being sexy is learning and loving how to be alone. Solitude is an important aspect of self-appreciation. I did not realize that until I was able to experience it for myself.

Usually, I get constant validation and attention from the multitude of followers on social media. Anytime I search for love, I can tap into a livestream, anywhere in the world via Instagram, or LinkedIn. However, one Friday night, I had just come home from a week in Hollywood where I had been taping a reality TV show, and my energy was higher than usual. Sounds glamourous, right?

It was, but I had no one to be with. I came face to face with loneliness. There I was—divine, sexy Devina—alone on a Friday night. I had finished all my work, talked to my parents on the phone, did yoga, played with fur babies, masturbated, and meditated. I used all my tools for self-appreciation and self-soothing. Yet, I was still feeling unsatisfied and restless. I craved a human connection.

Sure, it would be easy to choose to have sex with someone, but I understood that it would not lessen those feelings of loneliness. Sometimes, being by myself is better than choosing to spend time with just *anyone*. In the end, I spent time releasing my pain through journaling and writing about my sadness.

Acceptance of every emotion is empowering. I treated myself just as I would have treated a friend going through a rough moment. I gave myself kindness and support. I gave myself love when I was lonely. I invite you to befriend yourself in the same way. Coming face to face with undesired emotions is uncomfortable. Unless these emotions are acknowledged and accepted, they are guaranteed to resurface at inconvenient times. I have found that most growth and subsequent transformation happens in our darkest times. The journey towards a sexier version of yourself means staying in tune with all of your emotions. Time alone helps you identify *who* you are, without the distraction of other people.

What Is Conditioning?

Conditioning is the collected beliefs from your past, your history, and your ancestors who may have left their energies behind. It is important to let that go. In order to stay in a constant state of zero, you must release what does not belong to you. It takes a lot of mindfulness, soul work, and self-searching to discern how our conditioning affects us. There is not one set formula for this work; however, I created the exclusive K.A.U.R.™ process to help you on your journey. (You will discover more about the trademarked K.A.U.R.™ process as we move further on in the next chapters of this book.)

Often, people are not aware that their behaviour is a reflection of the way they were raised. When I catch myself getting upset at my daughter, I pause and contemplate my actions. I realize that it is not me who is angry or upset at her, it is the way that I was raised. My parents have successfully passed on so much of their baggage to me that I occasionally do to my daughter what they did to me.

In my case, for the longest time I was not aware that I was behaving in a certain way. I remember one time that I fat-shamed my own daughter using the same language my parents used on me. My daughter, Anahat, was eating candy after candy. I could not control the words that came out of my mouth. I told her, "Stop eating so much, you are getting fat."

To this day I am still upset at myself—how could I say such words to her? I was expressing the exact demeaning tone of voice and feelings of invalidation I grew up with. These words were a product of the way I was raised. They were my *conditioning*. I was not living my life in them, but my parents' lives. It was not mine, but their mindset that I was passing on to my child.

I allowed myself to become aware of my conditioning, so I could change my behaviour. I was able to let go of my past baggage, my childhood blueprint, and my conditioning to empower myself. When I did this, even once, it opened up new possibilities. I could share my stories, vulnerabilities, and addictions. As we continue on, I will talk further about my relationship with my parents and what has allowed me to forgive them.

Activity: Chapter Zero

Think back to your past, every day you have experienced up until today. What story keeps showing up that has not served you? What do you need to release to be at zero?

_____

_____

_____

_____

_____

Negative energy can be transformed to work for you! Where has most of your negative energy stemmed from? Select all that apply

○ Love & Relationships

○ Work & Career

○ Community

○ Friends / Family

○ Body & Self-image

○ Religion / Spirituality

○ Health & Wellness

○ Motherhood / Fatherhood

○ Finances

It's time to be the author of your life! Are you ready? Be bold, be honest, and ambitious—no holding back!

What would make you feel completely fulfilled? What does your Sexy Brilliant future look like? The more clearly you can describe it, the more easily you can attain it!

_____

_____

_____

_____

Chapter One: Too Fat

I am the fattest I have ever been; between depression, heartbreak, overcoming food addictions, and getting older, the weight just does not seem to come off. Yet, I enjoy my body.

That is a radical statement! I was raised to distrust my own instincts and have constant self-doubts. I have been told my whole life that I'm "too fat." I was always "too much." No matter what I offered, and no matter my natural gifts, I felt rejected because I did not fit the cultural ideals with which I was raised.

The cure for being "too fat" was to reclaim my body, my pleasure, and my desire for myself. I had to tell myself, "*This is my body, for me to enjoy as I wish.*"

Being sexy is more than just your physical self, although that is certainly a part of it. *Sexy* means daring, *sexy* means brave, *sexy* is radical self-acceptance. Being *brilliant* is about shining like the beautiful diamond you are and owning your intelligence. The Sexy Brilliant™ movement combines the subtlety of what it means to be sexy physically, mentally, emotionally, and spiritually with the brilliance of what is uniquely your own personality and your beautiful mind.

Sexy Brilliant™ is a global revolution that empowers all people to live authentic, powerful, fun, and fulfilling lives by removing toxic shame and striving toward higher consciousness. Sexy divine beings make friends with every part of themselves. You engage in self-work, constant self-study, and self-love, leaving behind any shameful pieces of your cultural heritage. Sexy Brilliance requires that you choose to abandon societal expectations in order to connect to your inner divinity and spiritual, sexy voice. Reaching your divine destiny is your birthright.

Inheriting Insecurity

My birth culture's considerations did not make allowances for my self-esteem. I was born in India to very traditional Punjabi parents. I spent most of my formative years in India. I lived there until I was twenty-three years old, and as a result, that way of life has seeped into my whole being.

India is still a very conservative country in many ways. I was raised to behave like a "lady." I was scolded if I laughed too loudly or if I was too outspoken. Since the personality I was born with can be described as quirky and flamboyant, I had to change my authentic self and behaviour to fit in. I always felt like I was not good enough because I could not possibly live up to those cultural expectations and the high pressure to fit in.

In India, and in many other traditions, one is taught not to question one's parents, elders or authority in general. One is taught that authoritative figures are always right. Like many of us, my parents' approval and blessings form a big part of who I am.

Those two opposing desires created massive discord within me. As a rebel eager to grow and spread her wings, I was very conflicted. I knew I was meant to do more than behave ladylike, and be the typical, proper, Indian daughter. To be honest, though, I pushed those boundaries very hard. I questioned everything my parents would tell me about my education, my clothes, my relationships, and my friendships.

However, when it came to body image and self-worth, I really bought into what they said: I believed I was too short, too fat, too ambitious and, therefore, unlovable.

For most of us, our families' opinion is the most influential as it comes from the most important relationships we have. Although I grew up in a home full of love and laughter, I was raised by two people with very conservative values. My parents were—and still are—strong role models. They are the ideal, in their culture and otherwise. They are overachievers who have succeeded through their hard work. They have been married for over forty years. My mother was a teacher and later an entrepreneur. On top of this, she ran the household, smooth as silk. My father worked for the government and wanted the same security for me—which is a real joke. Devina the diplomat? Ha! I am too unapologetic about myself and too outspoken to make small talk and negotiate diplomatic contracts. From day one, I was a brilliant misfit—a rebellious, free spirit who was outspoken, brash, and creative in my eccentric ways. I could not be more different than my parents.

Our daily dinnertime conversation was always about grades, school, and current projects. As a family, our exchanges focused on money, plans, and careers. We talked incessantly about our current achievements and our future aspirations. We were pretty much your typical Indian family, which means that we also compared and measured ourselves against other families.

The compulsion to keep Punjabi tradition impacted me profoundly. My parents had strong opinions on everything, from finances and careers to comparing ourselves to others. I would never measure up, and it made me miserable.

In school, I struggled with learning disabilities. My work suffered as my high intelligence clashed with below-par assignments. I never understood why I had to learn square roots in math... like, how could it help me solve problems of global hunger and caste system and the divide specifically in India? We were taught that all are equal, however in reality, this was not practiced. I found it disheartening, and my rose-coloured glasses were broken early on. I was a square peg in a round hole.

At home I came up short, too—literally. My parents compared me to tall and skinny girls. Instead of feeding me better, more nutritious food, diets were their prescription to help me lose weight. In retrospect, a lifestyle change to whole foods and less dairy may have helped, but their focus was on the volume of food I consumed.

They said I ate too much, and that's why I was too fat. Or, the problem was that I didn't exercise enough. *That* was why I was fat. On and on it went.

I believed what they said, because, as children, we believe the messages our early caretakers teach us. I was told repeatedly that I was too fat for anyone to marry. *Men only like skinny girls.* So, because of my big size, short height, and disproportionate weight, the message I got from my family as a thirteen-year-old and later on as a seventeen-year-old was clear: I was unworthy of love because of my weight and size.

This cultural bias is prevalent in many societies, and it can have a lasting impact on our self-esteem. I truly believed that I was unlovable because I did not fit the mould for what the culture and society considered attractive. At that time, I did not realize that attractiveness isn't defined by size, skin colour, sexual orientation, or how short or tall a person is. Later, I will share the tools that helped me overcome this teaching.

Family Influences

After repeatedly hearing I was too fat, I became very body-conscious. I always dressed in loose, unflattering clothes to avoid attention to my plump body. I was raised strictly to be modest and to not show my body off. You were supposed to cover up, both in public and even in private.

In my early years, I went to an all-girls school and

wore a school uniform. After the age of eleven, I went to a co-educational school. Altogether, I changed schools nine times because of all the travel and relocation that my parents had to do for their work.

However, despite all the constant changes, my parents were always there to take care of my siblings and me; my mother especially was the steady, unifying force behind our family life.

I also spent a lot of time with my grandparents, who instilled many of our family values in me. My paternal grandmother taught me all the old wives' tales that I know, such as: "Don't cut your nails on a Thursday." (To this day, I never got a reason why!) My paternal grandfather taught me how to worry more. In fact, he is probably worried right now, turning in his grave and thinking about me writing this!

I was desperate for my family to approve of me and of my body. I had zero body-confidence or self-confidence because I was always the shortest and fattest girl around at family gatherings, at school, or in the swim club. Friends, family, and neighbours would refer to me as moti, a word in Punjabi language meaning chubby. It's a cute nickname for a baby, but not for a tween who was always hungry for food and about to stuff her face with bread. Little did I know that hearing such "endearments" would lead to a food addiction, and ultimately, the creation of the Sexy Brilliant™ Foundation.

A Bad Case of Bulimia

My loved ones' constant belittling was what led me to being bulimic. I remember being sixteen or seventeen years old and stuffing myself with food. Then, I swallowed laxatives, so that I would not gain an ounce of weight. I started purging whatever I had just eaten so that I would not get any fatter. I have struggled with eating disorders ever since adolescence.

I would like to point out that I place no blame for this

on my parents, my family, friends, or neighbours. Now, I understand that the damage was not their fault, but rather the cultural programming with which they had been brainwashed and that had been passed down to me.

Looking back, I spent many miserable years on different diets to lose weight to please other people. All I wanted was to be accepted. However, to be accepted in India, I needed to fit the ideal: thin, tall, quiet, and demure. That type of woman was worthy of marriage and societal acceptance.

The bottom line is, you start believing what you are repeatedly told. This includes the messages you tell yourself.

Consequences of Our Conditioning

The cultural conditioning you receive has real consequences, for you and for the next generations that follow. I am very sad to share that because I considered myself to be so unlovable and really hated my plump body, I do not have a single picture of myself during my pregnancy.

My nine-year-old daughter Anahat once asked me, "Mommy, can I see pictures from the time that I was in your belly?"

I had to tell her, "Mommy does not have any pictures of you in her belly."

"Why, Mommy?" she asked.

I gently shared with her how I had no self-love and body-confidence because of my weight. I was too ashamed of my body size to take pictures with her in my belly. Even in pregnancy, I compared my body to what I saw on magazine covers. I could not get myself to accept my body.

Anahat kissed my belly and said to me, "I love your fat belly."

I smiled through my tears. I gave her a hug and kiss, and said, "Thank you for choosing me as your mother."

Changing the "Too Fat" language in my life then became absolutely necessary, not only for my health, but for my child's. She deserves to be able to love herself and be happy. Children learn by example. If I did not break the cycle of cultural judgement, my daughter would have to deal with the same struggles I do.

I have not been perfect in this endeavour. One day, I saw Anahat standing in front of the mirror and talking to herself. She said, "I am so fat, I need to go on a diet."

Can you imagine? A child saying that! What messages are we teaching our children? For me, witnessing this was a life-changing moment. I knew I had to practice radical self-acceptance. It was unthinkable that my daughter could ever stand in front of a mirror and tell herself that she is too fat. Instead, I could change the message by choosing to be kind, by accepting what is, and releasing what does not serve me. Then, I would be able to show Anahat how to do the same.

So much of life's journey is about self-love and self-acceptance. But how can you have self-acceptance when society, and even your loved ones, bring you down? You suffer when the closest people in your life do not encourage you to love and accept yourself. No one teaches you that loving yourself just the way you are, with all your *imperfections*, is the most empowering thing you can do for yourself and for others.

Look around you. What you see is *normal*. What you see in the mirror is *normal*. You are *normal*. Do not let anyone tell you otherwise. Do not strive for unrealistic standards. What you should be doing is loving yourself and your body, just as it is made.

The sexiness that lives within you needs your help to shine. You must express that divine light so that you can lead a brilliant life. For many of us, this is not a matter of stepping into a pair of high heels or sexy lingerie— though that may be a start! Sexiness comes from a deep self-confidence and faith in the self that is free of shame.

True sexiness is freedom from the negative messages you receive from your parents, your culture, and even the people closest to you. It is liberating!

To nip self-criticism in the bud, I sometimes ask myself, "Would you talk to your friend that way? Your lover? Your sister?"

Of course not.

The toxic messages you receive over a lifetime, even from people who allegedly love and cherish you, can make your body and spirit sick. The work of becoming Sexy Brilliant is difficult at first, because it requires you to challenge your relationships with yourself as well as your relationships with the people who pour these toxic words into your soul. When you realize that you deserve better than nonstop criticism and second-class treatment, that realization is guaranteed to transform your existing relationships. How could it not? You confront the "way things are" and embrace your potential. Those people who are meant to be with you on your journey will understand and support you. They are along for the ride. Those who fight against your personal development and try to keep you small, subdued, or ashamed will not and should not last long in your life.

My road to empowerment confused some of my friends and scared my family at times. I have even scared myself as I learned to create and set new boundaries. I built the courage to put myself out there in the world and learn about myself through other people. At the same time, I worked at deprogramming myself from my cultural blueprint. These gifts, challenges, and opportunities have led me to a life filled with the kind of satisfaction I thought only existed in romance novels.

Uncovering your sexiness is a process that has its own natural progression. Nothing can grow without clean water and pure light.

Imagine drinking dirty water your whole life. What would your first sip of clean, fresh water taste like? That is how I felt when I finally started providing positive, loving messages to myself. My body, which I used to think of as ugly, unattractive, and essentially bad, became beautiful to me. I flourished.

Denying my own needs and my sense of self was actually making me physically sick. Healing meant I had to dig deeply into a self and a body I had denied since I was very young.

I discovered my sexiness slowly. I did not understand that it was a power I was born with. The strength and courage to be sexy must be built, from the inside out. This starts with zero: with yourself, in your deepest core. You can begin this building and re-building process by changing the way you speak to yourself about your body.

I realized that I could change the messages I learned by giving myself nurturing, loving words instead. I could reclaim my body, my sexiness, and my divine nature. This was not work that I started lightly: it was a life-saving practice.

I discovered my hunger for self-love after my divorce. I thought my world was ending. In a way, it was. Everything I clung to, or by which I measured my self-worth was taken away. I was totally depleted of every resource that had both supported and starved me of genuine love.

I had to adapt and grow into my own power—now called sexiness—and learn to love myself, or die.

Often, you discover your true self in adversity. That was certainly true for me. The end of my marriage was the end of many things. It was a dramatic transformation that separated me from my expectations for myself, as well as the image my family held up for me as an ideal.

The marriage was arranged, according to my culture's tradition. When my marriage failed, I had to face the fact that all the messages and guidance I had received— well-meaning or not—were toxic for me.

I was in my early thirties, fat, single, and isolated. I went through a period of extreme depression that felt hopeless and unending. Waking up and getting out of bed was nearly impossible. All I wanted to do was kill myself. My self-esteem was at an all-time low. I was already struggling with my *too-bigness*. I blamed myself and my failures on who I was: a person who was *too fat, too loud, and too ambitious*. Now, I had yet another label to punish myself with: "divorced, single mother."

My shame, which I mistakenly thought was coming from outside of me, battered my self-esteem to pieces. I was in so much pain during this transition that I nearly lost my grip on myself. It took me some time to realize that those negative messages were not generated by my authentic, loving self. I had internalized them. They were not even based in reality. Nobody gets married to get divorced. Not many of us want to raise a child by ourselves, and not all of us want to live away from our families while doing it.

No wonder I felt like I was dying! My inner, sexy, divine, loving self was struggling to assert herself against these outside influences. To survive and transform into the person I was meant to be, I needed to totally reprogram the way I thought about myself.

The messages that I started giving myself were the opposite of what I was being told about being *too fat, too loud, and too ambitious*. Love was the antidote for the poison I had been fed my whole life. No matter how sad I was, I committed to looking at myself in the mirror every day with love, admiration, and compassion. I kept repeating to myself, *I am sexy*. I ignored the negative images and messages outside of me and reclaimed the gorgeous, sexy woman I knew lived within me. I decided that it did not matter that I had no food, zero dollars in the bank, and didn't know where the next job was coming from; I was not a failure. It did not matter that I slept on the floor on an old secondhand mattress; I was worthy. It did not matter that

I lived in this fat body; I belonged to myself, and I loved myself. The only thing that mattered to me was taking back my power. I never wanted to be at someone else's mercy—or feel *powerless*—ever again.

I wanted to be sexy. I wanted to be brilliant. I understood that if I did not see myself like this, nobody else would. I would continue to attract lovers and relationships who mirrored the self-loathing I felt, and who would thus treat my body with disrespect. That was no longer acceptable to me.

I imagined my future self. I knew I would be beautiful as I aged, because I connected to the core of my sexy self. I praised my features out loud. I told my dark brown eyes how they sparkled. I told my hair how perfect it was. I examined my nails and told them they were the most fantastic nails in the world. I didn't compare myself to anyone else, and I didn't ask anyone to compare themselves to me. I was allowed to be myself. I defined my worth for myself. I was growing and learning to love myself as a true spiritual being!

The more I repeated these body affirmations, constantly looking at the mirror and admiring myself, practicing not to flinch, learning to look into my own eyes, the sexier I felt. After thirty days, I had already noticed a significant improvement. After one year of constantly repeating these affirmations, they felt like second nature to me. I realized that sexiness, which is so often thought of as a purely physical quality, was an attribute developed by my inner work. I started to notice how sexy I really was.

The more I worked with my reflection and really looked at myself, the more I accepted my uniqueness. The more I was able to love myself, the more I found it easier to love others. I gave myself permission to love every curve, hair, wrinkle, and cell. Why shouldn't I? There is only one body in the world like mine, and it was given to me. I get to live in this beautiful body!

If ever I caught myself slipping back to my old patterns, I practiced being able to notice the negative self-talk, then pausing, and providing a loving message to counter it - *I am beautiful!* At first, before I was really in love with myself, I did this by stepping outside myself. I disassociated from my body and imagined it was not mine.

Eventually, slowly, gradually, I started feeling worthy of love. I would look at myself in the mirror and say: "I am lovable." I looked at my reflection and said: "You are so smart, so brilliant and so worthy."

The word *sexy* is such a taboo word in Asian culture, mostly associated with sex and not empowerment. Sexy is traditionally exactly the opposite of what I believed myself to be. My established cultural norms told me I was "too fat." Yet, here I was, rebelling against all those norms and allowing myself to love myself for exactly who I was: this fat, fluffy, brown-skinned woman with flabby arms, round belly, and saggy breasts. I would look at the mirror and repeat to myself: "You are so sexy."

And even: "Devina, you are *hot*."

Anytime that hateful little voice in my head started calling me fat, I stopped myself and repeated my loving words again and again, until I started believing that I was indeed sexy, daring, bold, beautiful, and desirable. If I still did not believe myself, I wrote the message down. The more I practiced being aware of myself and the little voice in my head trying to constantly bring me down, the more I got to know myself.

For me, accepting my whole self includes acknowledging and loving my big belly, my fat thighs, and my saggy breasts. It means that I am being me. I celebrate my size in my own unique and eccentric way. I totally make fun of myself to keep myself humble and light about my body. I love to play with my sexiness. I dress up, take glamour shots, and express my divinity and sexiness. This is how my mission to be Sexy Brilliant evolved. I am here to be my genuine self. I will never conform to the cultural norms of my past, the ones from the Eastern part of the world.

These negative, limiting messages cropped up every time I went through a period of growth in my journey to self-love. For example, a few months after my marriage ended, I was tired of feeling single. I had just come back from meeting some new friends I had connected with in a single parents' support group. We all had one thing in common: we were raising children on our own. The group was a great place to meet possible romantic connections.

Yet, I met no partners in my various social activities. I was a bit envious as I watched my single parent friends pair up and become couples. I quickly realized that I needed to find a way to meet men, too.

One day my mother called me from India and asked me what I was up to.

I, being brash, said, "Filling out an online dating application."

"Be very careful, all men want is to get naked with women," she replied.

Her discouragement made me very angry. "Mama, you don't understand. I also want to get laid."

That was the last time my mother asked me anything about dating.

Truly, it was not easy to put myself out there. It was definitely not easy to tell my mother that I wanted to have sex, for the sake of having sex, for pleasure and release. So often, women are told by our parents and the society around us that we do not and should not enjoy sex, or that only men enjoy sex. I grew up with both cultural and societal expectations, so it took me a lot of courage to stand up to my mother and take a stance not only with her, but also with the cultural programming that was still playing in my head.

I committed to caring for myself and told myself that I

deserved to be surrounded by love. Anyone who attempts to stop me from being *me* will be removed from my life and my circle. Do the same with anyone who is stopping you from being *your* own beautiful self.

The fact is, I wanted to enjoy sex. I had waited more than thirty years for an orgasm with another person. I wanted to get to know my body. Why was I constantly being told *not* to seek pleasure? I remember thinking to myself: *Pleasure is not a dirty word.*

To find the kind of pleasure I wanted, I not only had to get out of my own way but I also had to step away from the constant messages of disempowerment. Part of that project meant putting myself out there. I started paying more attention to social cues of people around me. Working with intention, I enjoyed and understood the information I was receiving and gathering about the way people interact as loving, sexy, brilliant human beings.

Getting naked and displaying confidence is a challenge. As a plus-size woman, I am now comfortable being called fat. I get called fat all the time. But, why is fat a bad word? Do we mock thin people?

Yes, I am not the average size. I am top heavy, and my body is somewhat disproportionate. I have thought about surgery to reduce my breasts. Plenty of women I know think the opposite. They want breast enhancement surgery, but not me. I have struggled with an odd body shape all my life. Most human beings (ahem, mostly men on dating sites) are more impressed by my sexiness than by my brilliance. Sexiness is so often thought of as only physical, but in truth, sexiness also comes from our inner work.

It has taken me a long time to accept my size. My confidence came in spite of tremendous pressure to stop loving myself. I did not always notice my own strength, because I was so quick to point out my own flaws. I finally began to realize that there is strength in loving and accepting all parts of myself. My imperfections are perfection.

My strength also comes in owning the days I want to give up, noticing when I get triggered, and accepting when I am plagued by my insecurities. I can feel the shift inside of me and the energy moving. Sometimes, I cry. I feel sad, worried, guilty or even angry. After letting those emotions sweep through me, the pain is released. I get up and keep moving. I continue living another day. I can feel good about taking all the parts of myself with me. Has it been easy? No, absolutely not! But it doesn't have to be difficult, either. Everything just *is*.

This world has tried to keep you from the truth of your being. It has discouraged you from self-acceptance and from welcoming yourself favourably. The reality is that you should be loved and accepted just as you are. Who you are is not purely good or bad; you are perfect and real, just as you are. Each person has a special uniqueness; that is your gift, too.

Perhaps, like me, you have grown up around people who fed you mixed messages. Remember, it's not their fault; *they* probably learnt those ideas from their peers and from generations past. Breaking those cultural cycles is possible when you decide to be real with yourself. You must share your authentic self with the world! That love starts with self-acceptance—of your own body and mind just as they are and not as you are told they should be.

Activity: Chapter One

Being real is often unacceptable in our culture and society. You are conditioned to doubt yourself and hate your body, without even realizing it. Where do you believe your conditioning came from?

On a scale from 1-5, rank the words below. 1 is the most probable source, 5 is the least likely.

#
_____ Friends or Family

#
_____ Intimate Relationships

#
_____ Religious Leaders

#
_____ Teachers or Bosses

#
_____ Media, Other

You can quickly become more committed to your cultural programming than to yourself. Why do you think this happens?

_____

_____

_____

_____

In your life, who has had the biggest negative impact on your self-image?

_____

Are you ready to forgive them? Why or why not?

_____

_____

_____

_____

If you are ready to forgive them, commit to a specific date!

_____

Chapter Two: Too Loud

I am who I am, and all the experiences I have had serve my purpose. I'm a woman with a message to share. I'm way too loud, and I love it! I have something to say to the world, and I say it. In speaking up, I choose to practice real honesty in my life. I wouldn't want to change myself for anything and anyone except for myself and my own growth.

The goal of the Sexy Brilliant™ Global Revolution is to empower others through sharing our struggles and removing toxic shame and the stigma associated with sex, addictions, being overweight, disability, mental health, and anything that is perceived as different that keeps us at low frequency. Instead of following damaging, old patterns, it's time for all people to empower each other—especially women. Now, more than ever, women must come together in sisterhood and support each other in any way we can. Women can be sexually empowered and enjoy sexual release for what it is: pleasure. Men don't have to be all macho, or mask their emotions; being able to acknowledge one's feelings and express their emotions is a strength—not a weakness.

What Is "Too Loud"?

Do you believe a woman can be too loud?

India is incidentally the country I was born and raised in. It does not value outspokenness. In the Eastern part of the world, tradition and upbringing are supremely important. However, I was not born to fit that mould and emulate those expectations. My loud voice developed early in my life with my parents. Every time I wanted to share my thoughts freely, I was labelled as being mischievous.

My family home was warm, but it was confining, like a cocoon. I wanted to spread my wings and fly. If I had been a man, this might have been acceptable—not permitted, but at least tolerated. However, I am *all* woman, so outspokenness was forbidden for me. In my culture of origin, the more women are quiet, the easier it is to control them. The same was true in my upbringing. But those rules didn't work on me. I couldn't be silenced. I couldn't be controlled. I couldn't keep my mouth shut!

In South Asian culture, family, including extended family and elders, must be shown respect. For example, you are not allowed to talk back to your elders. You can't refer to any older person by his or her first name. You address them as *Sir*, *Madam*, *Auntie*, or *Uncle*.

My parents were rather strict about this. As part of my upbringing, I wasn't even allowed to call my nanny by her first name. The cook deserved as much respect as the army officer next door. You called the cleaning staff at home *Sir*, or the Indian way of saying big brother: *Bhaiya*. This is how my family still works. They are still very respectful, but we pay a price for it: the price of being inauthentic, living in fear of our elders, and thus abiding by cultural rules that control, silence, and limit natural expression.

I often have to oppose my family, especially when I reject the cultural programming and baggage they try to pass onto me. In spite of this, I still have an immense respect for the culture and beliefs that I was raised with. I have found equilibrium. It has taken a lot of personal work and confidence to stand up to my early caregivers while still owning my identity. This balancing act takes courage. I must continually stand up to the parents, families, and people around me in order to keep my sense of self and my sanity.

It means reversing a lifetime of programming. Decades!

As awkward or painful as it sometimes feels, I must be true to myself and my life mission. I am allowed to honour who I was and where I came from, while also creating space for the Sexy Brilliant person I am becoming, every day.

My test for whether I am living up to this vision is whether I'm able to speak my mind and stand up to my parents when they are wrong. I do my best to be both kind and compassionate toward their viewpoints—without compromising myself.

As I evolve and grow through my life experiences, I get to know myself, and discover new things about myself. I find that I'm more true to myself now. I also feel more empowered, and free from cultural pressures that would keep me silent. I respect my parents. Often, when we're together, they get overwhelmed by my lifestyle choices. The culture I live in now, in Canada, is so different from theirs. When I am with my parents I'm not "allowed" to dress in shorts or body fitting t-shirts and dresses. To them, showing my body in any way represents immodesty. I like wearing shorts! In the hot summer sun, I enjoy wearing a sundress, as I love feeling the sunlight on my skin.

It can feel like a battle of wills. My parents, especially my father, still try to control me and my daughter. They use fear-based negativity and attempt to make us feel inferior and small. They use this tactic when we don't fit into their norms and expectations. One common way they do this is by telling me that I'm a bad example for my daughter. They criticize everything, from calling out the way I dress, to telling me that my hair is too wild and not styled the way a proper woman my age should wear it.

My daughter notices these messages and is already internalizing them, as I once did. Recently, I told Anahat that I want to get my nose pierced. She looked at me with wide eyes.

"*Grandpa* will be very angry with you if you do that," she said.

Immediately, I noticed how her energy changed. She got anxious and nervous, imagining my father's reaction. It didn't matter that I wasn't going to see him for another seven or eight months.

I started laughing. I gave my brilliant daughter a hug and told her, "Mommy must do what is right for *her*." Later on, after speaking to my therapist, I realized that this is exactly how generational fear builds in our children. Through observing the behaviour of family members and caregivers, we are taught the implicit values of our culture. You don't need to have it written out for you. You know how you must behave to please the people you love. It's true, no matter when or where you were born. Those values are passed on from parent to child. It's not my father's fault that he wants to control me and the way I dress. It's how he has learned to be; it's his mindset, his cultural beliefs.

It's up to me to break the cycle and be conscious of my own parenting style. My values dictate my life. I'm not too loud for me, even if my outspokenness is out of place in the family that raised me. Therefore, if someone tries to put you down or disapproves of your authentic self, know that these beliefs come from their own outside influences and you must mindfully make space to be your divine self.

Seeking Healthy Validation

Though I was raised to be silent, embracing my "too-loud" self made my voice one of my greatest tools. It helped liberate my uniqueness, allowing me to show my true colours. As I grew up, I realized that outspokenness about sex, women, money, and other subjects was disapproved all over the rest of the world, too. Most cultures equate outspokenness with being *too much*. People who are loud challenge others. Raising your voice is a risky move. It threatens most people—and engages others.

Nobody wants to stand out on their own. Being loud can make you feel like a lone voice in a big, unwelcoming world. That is why so few of us speak up. We are raised to value our culture over ourselves. We get messages to curb our authenticity, to fit in, to be socially accepted, and to adapt to the norm. If not, we become an outsider, feeling like we're not good enough.

But nothing could be further from the truth. I found my true self when I moved away from my need to be accepted by the people close to me. I found healthy validation when I connected with my authentic nature, which is not defined by the way I was raised or where I came from.

Authentic can be best described as being true to yourself. It's about self-knowledge, self-acceptance, and listening to yourself. To practice authenticity, you must honour your own brilliance and live with inner confidence.

Like anyone else, I face life's challenges. One of my biggest challenges and greatest blessings is my loud, dramatic personality. My flair for the fabulous made me an outsider in a culture that values submissiveness in women, and it translated into a constant need for validation and acceptance from my loved ones, family, peers, and society. This insecurity started at a young age and continued throughout most of my life.

Validation is not a good or a bad thing. As human beings, we all seek it. One morning, I was walking from the parking lot into my office. I noticed the landscaper working on the grounds. Petra is a middle-aged, wrinkled woman, and as I said, "Hello" I noticed she had a tattoo that stood out to me. I immediately went to look at it more closely. It was a tattoo of a beautiful butterfly. I started chatting with Petra and complimented her on her ink. Petra smiled, said thank you, and told me I made her day by giving her this compliment.

I could not help but smile back! Petra's happiness made me happy, too. The point is that human beings, even strangers, want to be noticed, appreciated, and validated.

Showing Off

As a young girl, I was often told to be calmer and to quiet down. My parents always told me to stop showing off. Being the rebel that I am, naturally, I had to do exactly the opposite of what I was told. Underneath my rebellion, my insecurity festered because I could feel their disapproval. I didn't have healthy validation to feed me while I grew.

Today, because of inner wealth resulting from the personal developmental work I have done, I have a new understanding of validation. I know the truth is that the only validation we need comes from ourselves. Sexy Brilliance comes from being nourished, loved, and well-balanced within yourself. However, if you are taught that you aren't good enough, you're set up to constantly seek validation from others. This makes you do unusual, unnatural, and inauthentic things to fit in and to get approval from your loved ones and society at large. The cycle of self-shame and unhealthy validation becomes toxic, unless you can find a way to harness your own shadows and dark energy to make it work for a better you. In a later chapter, I will talk more about my own addictive behaviour in detail, which developed from my struggles to fit in.

Validation must come from yourself, not an external source. By transforming your challenges into blessings and making them sexy, you can free yourself from the need to strive for perfection. You can be where you are: you do not need to fit in where you do not belong.

Silencing My Gender

Sex is the highest taboo in any culture, especially in India.

Growing up, we spoke about sex amongst friends, but we were so afraid of being shamed and by being labeled as "easy" or "sluts" that we never spoke about it in public. Even though a lot of us in high school had boyfriends, we would never dare to mention that we were sexually active.

Sex is still such a taboo subject that talking about sexual education is also forbidden. We treat sexual health as if it's not as important as our emotional, mental, physical, or spiritual health. Forget about talking about sexual abuse: that's still a big taboo topic, too. Many of us who experienced sexual abuse suffered in shame and silence because of the cultural conditioning that would not allow us to talk openly about our pain. I will discuss this subject later.

As a result of shame and silence about sex, teen pregnancies within the South Asian community are more common than ever before. I recently came to know about a sixteen-year-old student in Canada who had to have an abortion without the knowledge of her parents. I heard about this story from a local schoolteacher, who called to talk to me about sexuality and health within the school system. The teacher, a mentee of mine, was very worried about teen pregnancy rates, and young women needing to repeatedly seek abortions.

Of course, having children should always be a choice. Although there are legal resources and methods to follow if you choose not to have children, single parenting rates are still on the rise. As a grown woman raising my own daughter, I still face cultural prejudice against women and against sex. Why? Because I'm not married. Ultimately, everyone should be able to be protected, safe, and free to discuss sex without the taboo associated with sexuality. This is especially true for young people.

When I talk about overcoming dating addictions in the media, I am shamed. I feel vulnerable and naked, however, I've worked relentlessly hard to accept myself and overcome my addictions, that I refuse to stay quiet about it. Opening up helps other people. Yet, some of my high school friends decided that my honesty was a turn-off. For them, it was okay to have sex as a fifteen-year-old. It was okay to talk about it amongst friends. However, as adult women, it was not okay to do the same things—and enjoy them. When I came into my own being, these same friends chose not to be associated with me any longer. It was not my actions that pushed them away, it was my attitude, my lack of shame, and my ability to be too loud. I wasn't going to stay silent, therefore I could no longer be accepted in their group, nor did I need their negative, moral condescension.

Some of these friends deleted me from their Instagram and other social media because they didn't want to be associated with someone who is so loud about taboo subjects. Talk about double standards. No wonder women are seen as being the worst enemies of women! The truth is that "empowered women empower women."

I speak about empowerment on a holistic level. What I bring to the table is too much of a culture shock for them. Clearly, they're not ready to be truly sexy. They prefer to stay in the cultural narrative they grew up in. That is a choice they make—I hope they make it freely. I wish them nothing but a way to find their own brilliance.

Loud and Proud

Often, our biggest gifts are also our biggest challenges. One of the ways I became sexier was to embrace my loud personality. As a full-time single parent, I work constantly to balance the masculine energy and the feminine energy at home. I also strive to do this in professional situations. I am always looking for equilibrium, which is a lifelong challenge. It is true even in this moment. Although my circumstances have required that I take the lead in my life, I was always ready to do it anyway. If I had to choose between following passively or leading actively, I would always choose action and passion. After the inner, personal growth I've experienced, I have come to know myself. I recognize that my yang energy—otherwise known as masculine energy—is stronger than my yin energy.

At work, I am responsible for making all the decisions. I wouldn't change that in any way. I would never give my power to someone else. Now, I am not a bully. *Aggression* is an imbalanced masculine energy. Unlike aggression, *assertion* likes to give direction and is action-oriented. Balanced masculine energy is assertive, not aggressive.

My masculine strength also lies in having valour and being fearless. Those are all words that I used to describe myself. This is who I am—masculine in my energy, yet undeniably a woman, part of the female gender. Part of my journey has been accepting that I lack more traditionally feminine behaviours. A well-balanced feminine person has more patience and empathy than I do. I have never been patient, but with time, I recognize that I can change that. I bring balance into my life by acquiring new skills that allow the expression of my yin and yang energies.

Some skills can be acquired through self-awareness. I am finding equanimity due to my work on myself; I have more patience than I did earlier in my life. The feminine energy is receptive, so I mindfully work on remaining open. That has always been something that I struggled with in relationships, including the relationship with my parents. Even on my hardest days, I found it difficult to receive money from them. I would not allow myself to receive anything I didn't feel I had earned it, whether it was emotional or financial support. My fierce independence eventually forced me to crack through my shell.

With practice, I began to embrace all of myself, evolving into the leader of my own life.

Redefining Weakness

As much as I love being the leader, there are days when it feels like too much of a challenge, and I just want to be taken care of. Truly! On days like this, I remind myself compassionately and gently that the rise of feminine energy does not mean the loss of masculine energy. Both feminine and masculine energy are needed for us to live in harmony with ourselves.

On the rare days when the presence of my yang energy feels like a challenge, I focus on the women warriors who came before me for inspiration: women like Oprah Winfrey, Maya Angelou, and Gloria Steinem. They have all been overachievers in their own lives. I would guess that someone, somewhere along their paths said these queens were "too loud."

On my weaker days, I want nothing more than a beloved encouraging me. I want to be nurtured. I want someone I love to tell me everything will be okay. Those magic words: "Even if it is not okay, you will be fine."

Often, I do not have this kind of support at hand, so I must become my own best friend. I talk myself into having the confidence I need. I encourage myself. I show up for myself. I am one hundred percent responsible for myself. And you can be too!

Practising Self-Care

Self-care takes an infinite number of forms. One of the most important things I have learned is to say *no*. When I say *no* to someone else, I am really saying *yes* to myself.

For a brief, three-week period in my life, I had a relationship with a guy named Martin. Martin was a very sexy man and CEO of a company, but he struggled with extreme pessimism. Everything in his mind and outlook was always very negative. As brilliant as he was in his rational mind, he was emotionally bankrupt.

I quickly realized that if I were to continue getting deeper into this intimate friendship, I would not only be carrying my own emotions, but also his lower-frequency ones. His world was always dark, whereas mine was always sunny. How did I get over this vulnerable situation without hurting anyone involved?

I did a lot of self-talk and acceptance about Martin and our relationship as it was. I accepted that our energetic vibes were different, and therefore, not compatible or healthy for me. Even though the sex was great, I had to mindfully practice saying no.

- *No* to being with him.
- *Yes* to being alone.
- *Yes* to self-preservation.
- *Yes* to being "selfish."

You can say no. Learn to say no to people, situations, objects, and even food that bring you down. Have you ever been in a situation you did not wish to be in? Perhaps you had to spend time with someone who brought out your negative emotions. Imagine leaving that situation or that relationship without guilt. When you are Sexy Brilliant, you embrace your future self without fear or shame. When you say no to what feels wrong, you will be able to say yes to what feels right.

Someone can be wonderful, but not wonderful for us. Not everything will be the right fit, and not everyone is meant to be in our lives. Holding onto something because you feel you should is unhealthy, and certainly not sexy. Learning to say no to situations and people is also true empowerment and a form of freedom and self-respect. It is self-empowerment. It is a *yes* to yourself.

Building Self-Respect

You must know and internalize the message that you do not have to tolerate disrespect from anyone, especially yourself. Before I began knowing and loving myself, I was so unkind and disrespectful to myself. I could not look at myself in the mirror without saying hateful, degrading things. Even thinking about the unkind way in which I spoke to myself gives me the shivers. Changing those messages to loving, respectful words was a big step forward in my personal development.

When I became aware that I was being disrespectful toward myself, I was able to change the hurtful words I was saying. I use mindfulness to identify these times, and I gradually and gently change my mindset. If you have no respect for yourself, how can you expect others to respect you?

The more you know and accept yourself, the more inner confidence and self-love you gain. Your emotions, desires, and darkness are all part of you. In my case, I learned that I can embrace the fact that I enjoy showing off. I share this to help others identify and know their passions. Know yourself so you can live your truest self-expression! For me, self-love means loving all parts of myself, including the flamboyant part, the part that loves to have my picture taken, and the part that likes to be the center of attention.

The more self-love you have, the more love you share with yourself and others. *Love* is the answer. Remember, each of us is the superstar in our own lives. Knowing yourself and loving all of you is what frees you and allows you to be Sexy Brilliant.

The next time you look at yourself in the mirror, you can practice being kind and compassionate. You can admire your body, your sexiness, and your brilliance. You can admire yourself the way you wish others to admire you. Sexiness is often seen as a purely physical trait. It is great if that is how it starts, but it can also develop by beginning on the inside. Confidence is sexy. Intelligence is sexy. Common sense is sexy. Instead of feeling unlovable and alone, see how you are surrounded by like-minded, Sexy Brilliant communities.

I live authentically because I live in love. Now, as I pass by a mirror, I notice myself in a different way. I look for something positive to compliment myself on. I sometimes blow kisses to myself. I repeat the mantra I shared in the last chapter: *I am so sexy. I am so smart. I am so brilliant. I am so Sexy Brilliant.*

The more I repeat those affirmations, the more I believe in them. My self-esteem grows. I actually admire myself every time I walk by the mirror, instead of picking out something to hate. Try it. Compliment yourself. Blow kisses! You can appreciate yourself without waiting for someone to do it for you.

When you love yourself from the inside out, the same feeling shows up in how you carry yourself. When you perceive yourself to be sexy, others see it, too. Even better, when you are whole and complete, you worry less about seeking external validation. The approval of others becomes less consequential to your happiness. When you have self-respect and healthy self-esteem, you will never, ever again tolerate disrespect from others or from yourself.

As a young girl in my mid and late teens, I worked as a teacher's aide. By the time I was seventeen years old, I had opened up a kindergarten school with the help of my parents. For five years, I ran, taught, and managed the school. The work pushed me to connect to many aspects of myself: my inner child; my strong, powerful inner businesswoman; and my ambitious side. And when an opportunity showed up, I moved to Canada without any hesitation.

Even today, I look back to my days at the school I worked at as one of the most blissful times of my life. I was a girl then, so happy singing and dancing with young children. Now, whenever I can, I spend time with children. I make it a priority. In 2017, I volunteered at orphanages in Guatemala and India. The following year, I also spent some time volunteering in Rwanda. I was fortunate to spend time with children in all these places. Because I am a woman who speaks when inspired by my inner child, I most easily connect with children. This helps me stay aligned with my own life philosophy.

Children see the parts of you that you have forgotten or may have neglected. They understand beauty in a way that adults do not. Their pure expression, perspectives, and happiness are to be encouraged. I aspire to be more childlike, and to let go of the stress and fear that once controlled my every action.

Free expression is, well, liberating! Children understand this and do it naturally.

Flower Power

When you see me on social media or on television, you must have noticed that I wear flowers in my hair. People often ask me why I do this. My Sexy Brilliant answer is that flowers are healers. They heal with their fragrance, their colors, and their vibration.

Because I have such a colourful personality, I like to parade myself and be different. Thanks to my ongoing personal development, I know that flowers in my hair suit me because they make me stand out. Sexy, beautiful, and attention-grabbing. Right? Just like me, those flowers love to be looked at, enjoyed, and celebrated. That is what they were made for!

My pretentious side, like my loud voice, is neither a

good thing or a bad thing. I choose to look at it as a gift. I consider my flamboyance as a part of my passion to show others what I love, both about myself and about the world. I have always been like this, even when I was very small.

In embracing your passions, you can be authentically *you*. My passion is writing and telling my story, because I hope it gives you the courage to be unapologetically yourself. I hope you are moved and inspired to follow your passion and your dreams. You deserve to have meaning in your life. You are Sexy Brilliant.

My wish is that everyone is empowered and encouraged to know their true desires and wants. As I continue on my journey, I am more and more convinced that I am doing the right thing by following my inner voice and my own, winding path. I have taken the first steps toward self-love, and that makes me stronger and more confident as I pursue my calling.

The more you listen to your instincts, the stronger they get.

Receiving Constructive Criticism

Part of practising self-love is choosing who is close to you. You can have a higher standard for your inner circle. You are a reflection of the company you keep, and your tribe is your mirror.

If you do not love your friends, why spend time with them? You are drawn to people you genuinely want to be with. You attract what you put out into the universe, so when you are living your Sexy Brilliant soulful life, you will naturally grow to be with people who are like you and support your way of being. When those friends point out a quirk, flaw, or harmful behaviour in you, you can understand that they are doing it to help you. You can listen to what they have to say and see how you can use that information to improve yourself.

In my case, my friends criticized my dating behaviour.

I remember they were aghast when I told them I was looking for dates on Craigslist. Little did I know that it was an addiction, and I was getting a high from this virtual, anonymous messaging behaviour.

My girlfriends and I were sitting by the fireplace once, talking, and I mentioned that I was starting out a relationship with a man I met on Craigslist. They were dumbfounded and very judgemental. But for me, this behaviour was my "normal." I felt confident in my decision because I trusted my instincts.

I listened to my friends' reactions mindfully. Then, I told them that I felt good about my choice. I explained that I had only ever met beautiful souls, wherever I went.

My friend Anne understood my perspective, pointing out: "That is because you only see the positive in all situations."

Hate Mail

Every time I put myself out there, the number of hate messages I receive goes up—a lot! Anytime a woman becomes loud and outspoken, she is perceived as a threat. This is because a woman who knows, accepts, and loves herself is powerful.

One fellow wrote to me, "*You are fat, yet you're very sexy. If you're interested in performing live sex shows, I can help you reach a lot of men and make easy money.*"

I laughed a lot at this email. Receiving this message was the highlight of my day. Of course, I do not have anything against anyone who willingly uses their body to make money—that is their choice. People do live with free will!

Instead, I laughed at this email because my daily goals are to laugh one hundred times a day and also be the happiest person I know. I laughed because the truth is that a woman does not have to choose between her sexual side, her emotional side, and her ambitious side—or any other side, including her spiritual one.

I could have chosen to be offended. I could have allowed him to cloud my opinion of myself. It's in moments like these that we must remind ourselves that no one can make us feel anything we choose not to feel.

Most people are so used to labels, so used to being put in boxes, that an email like the above could be very offensive and hurtful to them. Somewhere we have lost our sense of self; we must remember that labels strangle the self and kill sexiness. If you live in those boxes, you end up no longer knowing who you are. If I had received this email that called me fat a few years ago, I would have certainly spent the day crying in front of my therapist. Instead, I am free of negativity: my own and other people's. I choose to release all these labels. I release the control others have over me subconsciously. I release other people's baggage. Hateful messages do not bother me because they are not about *me*. They are about the people who send them.

When someone takes the time to share hurtful, hate-filled, obnoxious messages, it is (sadly) a reflection of how they feel about *themselves*.

The more I know myself, the more confident I become in my being. I know that I am a loud, fun, vivacious woman. You too, are whole and complete as you are. Don't listen to all those repeated messages that make you feel weak and at a lower energy level. Further on, I will share more tools about empowerment.

Loving myself made me immune to others' hate. Yes! Self-acceptance, which comes from self-knowledge, is a revolutionary act. The more you accept yourself, the more you love yourself. The only hate that can hurt you is the hate you show yourself.

You are divine light...and no hateful message can change that.

I Am My Own Beloved

Everyone deserves love and belonging. Of course I want love, but I have come to the decision through a lot of darkness that I definitely will not get it by disrespecting myself. That is why I had to choose to release myself and my energy around so many relationships. I am my own beloved, and I love myself before I engage with any other person. Self-love allows us to maintain respect and healthy boundaries in all other relationships.

Yes, you deserve to love. You deserve to *be* loved. But why should you make yourself vulnerable to another person's disrespect? Are you looking to find yourself through your relationships? Freedom is defining yourself, on your own terms. If you would like more love and a greater sense of belonging in your life, the solution is self-love. Give yourself love. Give everyone around you love. You are love. *Be love.*

Instead of waiting for a partner to give you love, you become love.

One summer, I was at the outdoor organic market. I saw these wonderful handmade scarves and said to myself, "I wish I had a boyfriend who could buy me that green scarf. It would look so graceful on me."

I felt sorry for myself, sighed, and continued on my way. A few minutes later, my heart said to my brain, "Wait a minute. I do not need a beloved to buy me this pretty green scarf. I can give myself exactly what I want."

This was a very small step toward my own self-respect. I chose to give myself a gift and the love I deserved. You can give yourself gifts instead of waiting for others to offer them. You can treat yourself the way you would treat a partner, with tenderness and loving care. You show up for yourself.

The choice to love myself is bigger than a pretty scarf. It affects my relationships as well. Yes, I was selfish when I decided to let go of Martin. I was selfish because I put my self-care first. I had two choices: to drown in pessimism with him, or save myself. I chose to save myself.

You have permission to be selfish. Yes, you read that right. You can be selfish, and you need not worry about other people and their opinions. What other people think is less important than what you think of yourself.

Patterns of Struggle

When I left Martin, I made a mindful choice to prioritize my relationship with myself. I have done that in other areas of my life, choosing to accept all of myself—even my loudness. I consciously choose to prioritize addressing what I have struggled with. Every day, I work to know, accept, and love myself just the way I am.

I have a struggle pattern. It's a pattern of finding a situation, job, or relationship that is "good enough," but then I start feeling trapped and constrained. I struggle because the comfort zone I choose to stay in may be "good enough," but for me, it is never enough.

My relationship with Martin was not enough because I knew there was more for me. I could not stop with him, because I knew and believed that my future was more sexy and more brilliant. Not settling was a way to honour that calling.

My search for my purpose felt like it would be never-ending until I discovered and developed the Sexy Brilliant™ Global Revolution. Then, my desire for "more" felt satisfied. I came home to Sexy Brilliant, and Sexy Brilliant embraced me. Finally, I was free from the cycle of self-criticism, seeking outside validation, and settling for less than I deserved.

For many years, I sought approval and love outside of myself, thinking they would make me happy and fulfilled. You know what? All my relationships left me with life lessons, fun experiences, and meaningful memories. Did they satisfy my deep craving for love and acceptance? *No.* As soon as I realized that love and acceptance come from within, I was liberated. Self-love freed me and helped me to enjoy being myself again. I choose to forgive myself for the choices I made in the past and accept that my past experiences make me who I am. In no way do they stop me from growing and thriving.

I choose to see the glass as neither half full nor half empty. I see it as overflowing with love and laughter. You can, too. There is so much to look forward to. My past is a part of my future, but the future is now, at this moment. I am here and now, in this being.

Wouldn't you agree, that is rather sexy?

Activity: Chapter Two

Developing the courage to speak out and defend your beliefs can take a lifetime. The good news is that becoming outspoken does not need to happen overnight. Not everyone's bravery is expressed the same way. You can be assertive without saying a word. Assertive acts can be seen, not just heard!

Describe a situation where your actions spoke louder than your words.

_____

_____

_____

_____

What was the result?

_____

_____

_____

_____

What did you learn from this experience?

_____

_____

_____

_____

Owning your power also means choosing which battles are worth fighting. Only engage in those that are worthy of you! Think of a time when you continued to fight a battle that was not worth your energy.

_____

_____

_____

_____

What advice would you give to a friend who was in a similar situation?

_____

_____

_____

_____

Chapter Three: Too Ambitious

I write about the dance with the ego very often. And I used to believe that destruction was the only choice, now I know better... and it is not destruction, rather befriending the ego, and consequently having a loving relationship with the ego, that allows for a connection with the innate creator.

Like all of us, once in a while I let my ego take control. After getting used to the idea that I have an ego, I decided to name her Claudia. She is my second self and I cannot seem to get rid of her. Henceforth, I have decided to refer to her as my best friend.

After a lot of reflection, and many anxiety attacks around the subject of an ego, I have given Claudia the task of helping me take care of myself. She has become my ally. She empowers me to walk away from unhealthy situations, or situations that do not serve my best interests. However, we do not always agree. We have great debates!

Here is a typical dialogue between Claudia and I on the idea of relationships.

Claudia: "Stop trying to find a way out. It is so much easier and financially safer to stay with this guy you're dating."

Devina: "Hell no. The sex is awful! I'm not staying for that. Besides, it's an unhealthy relationship."

Claudia: "No, it's not unhealthy. It's just average, and average is acceptable."

Devina: "Not in my world, honey. I'm too brilliant for that."

There have been times when our talks have not gone so smoothly or decisively. At one time in my life, I would let

Claudia talk me into or out of just about anything. However, it's important to differentiate between reality and ego when deciding what you want in your life. Sometimes our egos like to play with us, and the ego's message should not always be confused with being "truth." Creative visualization is a great tool to use in discerning the difference, which you will practice in an exercise later.

Ego can be related to ambition. Some people are naturally more ambitious than others; it's possible to be self-loving, loud, and ambitious without being "egotistical." Ego can serve the self's higher purpose and, in turn, the world.

Gender and Ambition

An ambitious woman is perceived completely differently than an ambitious man. When men behave ambitiously, they are seen as being strong, clever, smart, driven, and doing manly things. When women behave ambitiously, it is usually not so kindly perceived or received. When women know what they want and how to get it, they get called "bitch," or "angry feminist," or even "bad mother."

I am too loud, so I stand up and assert that I am none of those things. I simply want to live my fullest life and do my best with my abilities, living kindly, and with respect for myself and others.

For years, I wondered what my purpose in life was. I underwent a relentless self-examination. Did I want to be what my parents wanted from me or live my own path? Did I want to allow my vagina to be used for others' pleasure, always receiving and never enjoying? Was I a revolutionary who would change the history of the world, or just a horny, single mother who cruised Craigslist personal sections as an anonymous user, hoping to get laid?

So many choices. So many options. So many men. In

the end, my hunger for life and my curiosity got the better of me. I chose to acknowledge my weaknesses and my addictions and share all of myself with the world. Yes, I am in recovery from a love/dating addiction. For years, I have used matchmaking websites, even looking for love by being a participant on Hollywood reality TV, and dating apps to find my worth. I am proud to say that I am now in recovery.

I have always been known as *Too Ambitious*.

Where does my ambition come from? I have to say, most of it is my gift from birth. The rest came from reading, learning, and always being open-minded. A few weeks after I had chosen the title for this book, I saw both Reese Witherspoon and Priyanka Chopra give lectures about their ambitions. Hearing two powerful women I admire talk about this cultural taboo immediately erased any doubts I had about the title of this book. Ambition drove me forward, but talking about it was considered unladylike. Like my fat body and my big voice, my ambition is an essential part of me. It's one of the traits that has shaped my life.

I have always been curious and a quick learner. Thanks to my parents and their financial commitment, I went to a private school. It was an all-girls academy and *very* Catholic. In my teens and my twenties, I was severely affected by this traditional, strict education, and its many rules and barriers. My curiosity was not encouraged, and my natural gifts were beaten down. As you may recall in the previous chapter, we spoke about my struggle with being too fat. I was not tall enough. I had zero self-esteem, and consequently, very little self-love. Once I was able to recognize that I treated myself poorly because I did not like or even love myself, it became easier to change that notion.

I said to myself, *Clearly, jumping from relationship to relationship, job to job, and career to career has not worked. What will? Can I become my own favourite person?*

Of course I can! This is where my story changed from fear into love.

As a woman in my thirties and a mother with a prominent business, the desire to know more has played a big part in my self-development. I follow celebrities, authors, gurus, and self-help wizards as well as everyday people. All of these people inspire me. By keeping my eyes and mind open, I have learned a lot about different cultures, religions, and practices.

I have also stayed open to different spiritual teachings, because that is how I can live with the most freedom, aligned with the highest good. I do not identify myself as a member of any particular religion. If I had to define myself, I would use the phrase SBNR: *spiritual but not religious*. I am a peace-loving warrior, but I also identify as a peaceful anarchist. The spiritual basis of my life upholds and supports my ambitions by allowing me to constantly reach for my highest vibration.

In vibrating at a high level, I attract, absorb, and offer nothing but the highest intentions for myself and others. This, in itself, is one of my greatest ambitions, but it was not always this way.

Full-Time Student of Life

Looking to change the language around female ambition, I revisited my family traditions and cultural programming. My upbringing exacerbated certain parts of my addictive personality, especially in the area of academic achievement. I have been a perennial student, collecting degrees and diplomas and pursuing new interests. I am always curious about learning and gaining more knowledge.

Part of this quest for learning has led me to leave jobs and situations that have not helped me grow. The degrees and training that I pursued have given me confidence and assured me that I am employable. After successfully getting more than 9 diplomas, I can confidently say that you should never let education get in the way of learning. You are brilliant in your own unique and amazing ways.

I failed high school. However, I would not let anything come in between me and my dreams. I would not allow my past failure to limit my future. So often, I have left jobs without having a back-up plan. Every time I willingly took a risk by leaving an unfulfilling job, things worked out. Yet, each time I didn't listen to my sexy inner voice, I made unwise decisions.

Your conscience is always guiding you. You may argue with your ego, but the more you listen to your inner voice, the stronger it gets.

Practical Ambitions

A couple of years before I created Sexy Brilliant™ Global Revolution of empowerment from the inside out, I met a new friend through my running club. We went out for dinner together. Fabian was a real estate investor and broker. He told me that I would do exceptionally well in the same field—exactly what I had repeatedly heard from my parents, friends, and business colleagues. After meeting Fabian, it was not hard to convince me to get yet another degree, this time in real estate.

As usual, with my relentless optimism, I set about making the change. One week after my dinner with Fabian, I signed up for a real estate course. In Canada, a real estate broker has to follow a special accredited program and earn a license to be a realtor. The nine-month course I embarked on was weekly and full-time. My goal was to learn about real estate and to improve my knowledge of property management, so I could take better care of my investments. I already knew that I didn't want to buy or sell real estate for other people; however, in view of the fact that my life was filled with so many transitions, I was open to any possibilities because I intuitively knew that there was something bigger than myself waiting for me.

Most of all, I was curious. I wanted to learn. I have found that unless I am really passionate about something (or someone), I lose interest quickly. Being passionate is also one of my gifts.

For some reason, I thought getting a real estate license would be easy. I mean, how tough could it be to get another college diploma? Wrong! I underestimated the time my new program would take and the stress it would cause me. It was like juggling ten plates in the air at once, without dropping any! I already had my hands full. Along with school, I was running my own business, and being the best possible full-time, single mom.

I was an incredibly busy, full-time student of life.

In spite of my very full life, I completed that diploma. I am super-proud of myself for never missing a single day of school. I always sat in the front of the class, close to my knowledgeable professors. I asked a lot of questions about anything that was not clear to me, even if I was self-conscious asking about things that may have seemed simple to some of my fellow peers. Although I admit to studying very little in most sections of the course, I did concentrate on the finance classes. It was nerve-racking managing it all: school, work, and being a conscientious mother. I *did* manage. I did it.

Towards the end of the program, when final exams and assignments were due, I asked my very traditional, orthodox parents who live in India to come and stay with me for a month. I needed their help because I found it nearly impossible to handle everything. My folks helped me care for my daughter, who was thrilled to have them around.

With their help in other facets of my life, I eventually passed all my exams, every single one. I did so despite my learning disabilities and the enormous amount of responsibility on my shoulders.

I learned a tremendous amount while studying this course. I learned what was on the syllabus, but also a lot about myself. I learned that I can balance my self-care and my activities in order to manage my stress levels. I do not need to agonize about exams. After all, I have been in one kind of exam situation or another a lot in my life. I am a keen learner. The proof is the number of diplomas I already have. The good news is that being differently abled (due to my learning disabilities) did not stop me; I even learned how to better manage my ADD. I thrived under extreme conditions.

I am very social by nature, and I love people. I knew this about myself already, but my real-estate school experience really cemented it for me. I learned to appreciate myself more. Learning differently is not a drawback. I believe it makes us gifted.

All in all, I had a successful time studying and ended my experience feeling truly empowered. I formed some friendships with my classmates and professors. They helped me flourish in real estate school. I succeeded in adding another diploma to my blossoming collection of certifications. In pursuing this degree, I also made choices that were aligned with who I am. I am constantly learning and constantly evolving.

But things change, and for me, transformation is a constant. After graduating, I decided that I didn't want to go back to a corporate career after all. The real estate world held no attraction for me, in part because I had worked in corporate finance for fifteen years already. The knowledge I acquired for my real estate license was valuable because it made me a better real estate investor. I could have moved forward with the plan I had made, but it did not feel right. There were other parts of my life that really needed my attention.

In the end, I had to make a choice between spending time on work or time with my daughter. With my already busy career, including reality TV, I chose my amazing, brilliant eight-year-old girl. After the final exam, I asked Anahat if she missed seeing me. She said, "Only a little bit."

I smiled. I love my daughter so much. She is the light of my life. Any ambitions that I hold or may have held at one time in my life, all lead me to being a better person and mother to her.

Pressure to Fit In

Life is defined by more than just your family background, nationality, and religious or spiritual orientation. You constantly have to figure out your place in society and in peer groups.

In school, that concept starts as the idea of popularity. Most people will not admit that they want to be in demand, desired, or popular. A person's popularity often comes and goes so fast that whether they are well liked or not, does not really matter. Read this week's edition of a top-selling magazine and then compare it with another one from last year. You can see the shift. Few people have enduring popularity. Most are just a flash in the pan.

Of course, I was the same as everyone else. I wanted to be liked, to fit in, and be popular. To do all this, I curbed my ambitious side because I never wanted to seem like a threat. Ambitious women are considered unattractive in our culture. The question is posed - Do women change themselves to fit into the traditional male-female dynamic?

This assumes, of course, that men do not appreciate ambitious women.

But, and there is a big *but*, the right men do like ambitious, successful, and powerful women. (I will share a little bit more about this in Chapter Six.) The same goes for anyone who might be reading these words: the right people will appreciate and have respect for your ambitions, your success, and your self-actualized power. For me in the present day, it means accepting that not everyone loves the ambitious side of my personality or my authenticity. I have lost many friends because I am seen as a threat to their comfort zone. I accept this and understand that their rejection is not a reflection of something that is wrong with me; rather, there is something in *them* that needs to be addressed. That process is completely out of my control.

When you hear the word "popular," your mind probably goes right to whatever cliques or established groups roamed the halls of your high school. Humans are social creatures, so this becomes one of our first ambitions. Popularity is part of your awareness, beginning early in your lives. Like it or not, social acceptance is what you crave for in order to fit in. Peer pressure causes you to compare yourself with those who are admired or popular, and maybe even a little bit feared.

For me, high school popularity or feeling envied or desired is not what being "sought after" is all about. To me, *ambition* means being true to myself and my gifts, regardless of whether or not they bring me popularity.

For example, imagine a woman who is nice to everyone. You might see her in the elevator at work every morning. She connects with people from all different cliques and backgrounds. She smiles at everyone as she walks through the office. She's not afraid to be who she is. She's confident and self-assured in her being, which makes her a life magnet. Though she's not necessarily the most ambitious or loudest woman in town, she's delightful to be around, because she's also connected to her inner child. Everyone likes this woman because she is genuinely a kind-hearted person, and as you know, kindness is contagious. That woman could be you!

I know that I try to be the best version of myself on a daily basis. I lead an authentic life, and for me, that is my goal. I have taken a lot of time working through new processes step-by-step, applying my inner strength, and getting out of my own way to become who I am today. This includes being open about my weaknesses, my personality and my genuine self, regardless of social influence or popularity. At this stage of my life, I live my purpose. I embrace my ambition without hurting anyone or causing any harm. How others judge me is their choice.

Defining Our Purpose and Success

Finding your happiness—your bliss—is your life purpose. This journey is not as easy as it may seem. Part of being an earthbound human is dealing with the expectations that the world has given you. That includes relationships and material success and how you define them, or how they define you.

Finding your purpose often comes at the cost of increased expectations. When I started my search for meaning, encountering the unknown brought out my insecurities. I started from a fear-based mindset, wondering if I would ever be good enough. This is normal, and once I realized where my fear was coming from, I was able to change the message from fear to love.

In reality, you can create your own success—and sexiness— by directing your thinking. In an abundance-based mindset, increased expectations lead to higher expectations. Growing and leveling up are continuous and powerful in this mindset. Commitment to self-love and following through on your ambitions creates an opportunity for growth in all facets of life. All you have to do is look within yourself and practice self-actualization through positive affirmations. To avoid making fear-fuelled mistakes, you must remind yourself that the only validation you need is the inner validation you give yourself.

Admit it: ego can make people feel like competitors. You might feel like you don't want others to have more success than you. You might want to be better than your friends, family, neighbours, colleagues, and so on. However, the measure of your success is how you treat others and what you do for the rest of society. Regardless of your ambitions, success on the outside begins with success on the inside.

If you really want to improve your outer world—your health, your relationships, or your finances—you must first improve your inner world. The most effective way to do this is through the practice of continuous self-awareness. Self-love begins with self-knowledge and radical self-acceptance. As I mentioned in Chapter Zero, the goal is to always be at *zero*, a position of maximum stability.

No matter how many people like you, there will always be many more who find fault with who you are and what you do. This becomes clear and more evident as you level up and broaden your base of potential influence in the world.

Something to remember: financial wealth does not automatically mean that you are successful at life. *Success* also means being flexible, open, and non-judgemental. Taking this approach to life allows for a clear mind for making sound decisions. This is true for everyone. In business and in personal relationships, success requires constant assessment and reassessment of relationships, opportunities, and situations in which you find yourself. Success is not static, but dynamic: you can always re-adjust your approach as needed.

Taking Ownership

The first step to prioritizing and accepting your ambitious

side involves taking responsibility for your actions and decisions. You can take responsibility for yourself and your own happiness. It really is that simple. To be prosperous in life, you have to look at how you deal with life situations.

For example, one summer I was supposed to go for a bicycle ride with my daughter's foster grandmother, Gisele, and some friends. I showed up fifteen minutes late because I was so focused on writing that I lost track of time. Naturally, everyone was waiting for me and also became a little bit worried. I was extremely embarrassed, but by taking ownership of my tardiness and addressing it up front with my fellow riders, I took responsibility for my actions. Instead of getting upset and allowing myself to reach for excuses, I successfully took ownership for my part in being late. As a result, I had a lovely bike ride, we laughed at my expense and I'm still teased to this day.

Success is based on the ability to deal with the twists and turns of life and its perpetual flow of change. In my previous example, the late show-up was mine.

How adaptable are you? You're faced with many situations each day. It could be a recent break-up, a health issue, drama with a loved one, a job loss, or employment change. The common factor is that your life situation is constantly changing. Are you adapting to all of life's tests, turbulence, and flow? By taking ownership of your life's events instead of letting them or your emotions run the show, you redefine success.

To be able to advance and evolve, you need to learn how to let go, and apologize when you're wrong. You need to deal with the flow of change. Part of that process is that you often need to leave people, situations, and other things behind. Although it's difficult to know the reason why and to accept it, you should always believe that there are better things ahead of you than those behind you. Looking ahead, moving forward, and owning your future are just as important as owning your past.

Food for Ambition

What's the reason you wake up in the morning? What makes your heart pound so fast that you feel alive and want to conquer the world? Have you found that thing? Have you ever felt like that?

Finding your purpose and allowing yourself to participate in it is the most important thing in this sexy journey of life. Everyone dies in the end. Life's only certainties are paying taxes and getting stuck in traffic while you're here on earth. Living this sexy life is the only gift you have right now, all the time. Approach it with a grateful heart.

If today was the last day of your life, would you be proud of what you have done so far?

"Too Ambitious" could be another way to say "Too curious." My ambition has been a blessing and helped me find my life mission of Sexy Brilliant™ Global Revolution. I was not raised to be an ambitious woman, so it's not easy to leave my old, familiar role. It's not easy to stand up and say, "I am too ambitious." However, it's far more important for me to follow my passion, purpose, and excitement, than to try to comply with an outdated cultural expectation.

When I was younger, even though I was always searching for something and using my ambitious side, I wasn't comfortable sharing how I felt or what I desired. Many societies and cultures look down on women who are ambitious, because ambition is considered a masculine quality. Now that I am a leader and a mother, I advocate strongly for others. It's my responsibility to champion the power and ambition of young people, especially women and girls.

One morning, when Anahat had just woken up, she asked me, "Mama, can you teach me to be ambitious like you?" I remember my surprise at her question. I gently told her, "Everyone has different ambitions. The more you know yourself, the easier it is to live a purposeful life."

Anahat loved my answer. This question from my eight-year-old taught me that it's crucial to empower children, build their confidence, and encourage our little ones to speak up, so they feel validated. Change begins at home.

The new movement of an all-inclusive and empowered culture starts right now, with you and me and our community.

Uncharted Territory

I believe that the women's movement is still young. Our freedom is so new that women, and society as a whole, are still adjusting to the new dynamic. Around the world, relationships between men and women are changing as each sex becomes more empowered with better knowledge of the other. It's clearer than ever that there isn't one type of partnership that fits everyone. With the rise of the women's rights movement, the decline of traditional masculinity has changed our realities.

One common relationship dynamic occurs when women emotionally castrate men and men disempower women. This is not a new dynamic. Today, with global communication, awareness of this toxic problem is now widespread and mainstream. I have experienced it myself, and when I saw the same dynamic hurting other women, single mothers, and Indian families, I decided to face it head-on, using my own voice and life as an example of how to heal.

Many men have reached a point where they are unsure what their roles should be. The change in sexual politics can be disorienting for both men and women as well as for people of other genders. Men are stereotypically action-oriented; physiologically, women have been viewed as receivers. Many women these days are comfortable being equally action-oriented because of the sociological shift. Frankly, men often don't know what to do with women and are struggling to find their place in ever-changing, globalized systems. In changing gender roles, the dynamics of dating, mating, and relationships have changed too.

Feminism has greatly affected our world in every way, including with regards to technological changes and relationship imbalances between the sexes. What remains the same is that the feminine is always seeking connection; the masculine is always seeking perfection. Step by step, bit by bit, they move closer toward one another. I truly believe that when both partners bring equal strength and assertiveness to the table, it can and does only make male-female relationships stronger.

When we talk about empowerment, we often talk about empowering women. We centre femininity. Let's not forget that the other half of every person contains masculine energy. The male and the female are part of the same nucleus. The Divine Feminine's counterpart is the Divine Masculine. The world needs both men and women to step up and lead by example. This can become part of your joint ambition for yourself and for your partners, in both business and personal relationships.

Being ambitious does not only apply to your work life. In my case, ambition is a quality that I find attractive in my mate as well. An important part of becoming an empowered person is to embrace who you are, celebrate who you love, and find others who connect with you and appreciate your authentic self. That includes accepting your collective ambitions. As you explore who you are, you learn more about the kind of partners you want in your life.

Challenges Can Intensify Ambitions

A few years ago, I convinced myself that I should climb

Mount Washington, one of the highest mountain ranges on the Eastern coast of North America. I wanted to do this in the winter. So what if I had never undertaken something like this before? Inexperience was not going to stop me.

I took the first step before I had much time to think about it—one of the blessings of being a risk-taker. I sent my name in to a foundation whose charitable focus is to help single parents reclaim their sense of self through wilderness challenges. I received a response: I had been selected to participate in the climb with fifteen other single parents, from all walks of life. The foundation arranged training, equipment, and transportation for this incredible life experience.

Much of the training involved running up and down outdoor stairs with heavy equipment on our backs, sometimes in the snow and ice. I trained in all conditions, even when the temperature was -20 degrees Celsius. I didn't miss a single training session, and successfully completed the three-day winter ascent of Mount Washington in harsh weather conditions. I received lots of help from everyone around me.

I often reflect upon those stairs where we trained. Consider a staircase with 431 steps. This staircase becomes a metaphor for any challenge you face. It can seem insurmountable, and the path to the top is packed with obstacles. Many people might discourage you from trying, or even beginning. However, once you have decided that you want to reach the top, you begin to make the necessary moves. You push yourself. You practice. And you find people who help you.

As you continue taking steps upward, you get closer to reaching the top. Just imagine the view from the top when you have all that you ever dreamed! You will be able to look back and see all of those small steps that got you to where you needed to be.

First, you start with the decision to take the first step. Perhaps you are already ambitious and don't even know it. No one else can or will take that step for you. You're only going to be as successful as you believe you will be. Being ambitious is also being just daring enough to make one small move.

Open to Change

As our society shifts, people either learn to flow with it or be pushed along. When you're closed off to change, your struggle only intensifies. It's essential that you feel free, vulnerable, and open with your community. Opening up and being vulnerable feels scary at first; with practice, it feels liberating.

I am continually grateful every day to have a supportive community of amazing people around me. I share a lot, as being "too loud" is my gift: in other words, being expressive is my unique talent. A loving relationship with myself helped me leave behind my past and the blockages that have prevented me from being myself: a woman who is fat, loud, and ambitious.

I have had to move beyond family concerns, past relationships, and my old belief systems to get to the core of who I am. I have had to become familiar with my limitations, which means living in the knowledge of my darkness and accepting it, instead of constantly fighting it. This makes me feel extra empowered.

Everything that I have struggled with—such as my body confidence, self-image, relationships, self-love, learning disabilities, language issues, emotional expression, and addictions—makes my story valuable. Empowerment is a process. It is a journey to gain mastery over your own life. It means inner work, personal growth, and mindfully getting out of your own way. It requires radical self-acceptance, self-encouragement, and constant self-love.

Knowing all of yourself is the only way to becoming sexier. Self-knowledge is true empowerment, which also means letting go of the people who stop you from living your dreams. Feel free to banish all those people who hurt, belittled, mocked, discouraged, and upset you along the way. As your sexy energy is heightened, you too will notice that those who aren't on the same vibration level as you will no longer be a good match.

Self-empowerment starts slowly and comes back to self-love as well as self-awareness and self-regulation. Everyone has different timelines for their journeys; you need not judge others or compare. Rather, accept people as they are, on their own sexy journeys. It's crucial to recognize that everyone has a different path to take.

You are responsible for empowering yourself, and that's where your focus begins. You can encourage others who are going through their own transformation in a non-judgemental way. Sexy Brilliance is not something I can teach in a classroom; however, I will transmit what I know to you, so that you are empowered to know, accept, and love yourself. In the next chapter, you will begin the K.A.U.R.™ Process and build on what you have learned about being too fat, too loud, and too ambitious.

Activity: Chapter Three

Visualization is a powerful tool that I often use to work through my ambitions. I struggle to balance and clarify my desires. Often, I go through phases in my life. Sometimes, I feel extreme motivation for a worthy goal, then lose interest once I've achieved it. Other times, I might simply lose focus and aim for something new. It's important to be clear and bold with what you desire!

What are the non-negotiables in your life? Close your eyes and imagine what would sadden you to *not* achieve.

_____

_____

_____

_____

Now, think of all the things that make you excited! Make a vision board for your success. Add all words, symbols, pictures, shapes, colours, numbers, names, and other images that inspire you.

On a separate paper, create your vision board

Visualization is so powerful that sometimes it can disconnect you from reality. The key is to stay focused on your future, while also anchoring yourself to the present. Think of an important goal you had that was driven by "ego." What were the results?

_____

_____

_____

_____

Now, think of another goal you had that was driven by "truth." What were the results?

_____

_____

_____

_____

Your body has miraculous ways of showing you signs when you're driven by "ego" or when you're striving for something that is out of alignment with your purpose. Your body speaks to you in the most intimate way. Become aware of the signs and you will know when you are driven by truth or ego!

Circle all the physiological symptoms you felt when you maintained ambition for something that was not right for you:

Headache   _Shortness of breath_   _Indigestion_

Dizziness   _Sweaty palms_   _Rash_

Nausea   _Perspiration_   _Heartburn_

Any other signs that indicated your ambition was out of alignment with your purpose?

_____

_____

_____

_____

Chapter Four: In-Between

The moment when you realize you have a choice to make is known as the in-between. The choice can be large or small. Should I buy the black pumps or the camel ones?

Should I stay in the financial industry where I am unhappy at a soul level, or should I put that career and lifestyle choice to the side in honour of my greater life's calling to build the Sexy Brilliant™ Global Revolution? These are in-between moments.

Every day, you are faced with choices that define who you are and who you become. As overwhelming as this might seem—at least if you are a perfectionist like me—it's important to be aware that there is no right or wrong choice.

In this chapter, you will learn to honour the place between choices. In-between is the space where you have to allow yourself to just be for a while, as you find out what will serve you and your community at the highest level.

One Saturday evening, I was supposed to go on my third date with James. He was a sweet, short, stocky man who wore glasses. I had been seeing him for about a month. Instead of going out, I got stood up. At the very last minute, James cancelled our evening together. He said that his father's senior dog had died.

Although James's excuse was transparent to me, I was very understanding at the time, because acceptance of every situation is the highest form of empowerment. I was grateful that James let me know that our plans for the evening were off instead of flat-out ghosting me. The story he told me did not surprise me. Anyone who has done any dating will have heard one version of this excuse or another. Whether it be dogs, families, or last-minute work projects, James's dead dog story was repeated by different people in many different forms.

The truth is, I had really been looking forward to my third date with James, especially in view of the fact I had been celibate for the last few years. Naturally, I was very disappointed at the last-minute change of plans. However, you always have a choice to go with or against the flow of life.

Instead of feeling crushed by the cancellation, I changed the way I approached dating. At that moment, I decided to let go of expectations. It was, after all, my own broken hopes that hurt me the most. Instead of wasting precious time mourning the unmet expectations, I used the experience as an opportunity to grow. After the cancelled date with James, I decided to date with my focus on just having a fun night out with someone I genuinely liked. I chose to consciously leave my expectations out of it.

The cancelled date fell on a Saturday night. I already had a babysitter and I found myself all dressed up with nowhere to go. I could have sulked about James and his excuse, which felt like a personal rejection. Instead, I chose to use the time and opportunity to do something different all by myself. So, I took myself on a date. I left on my dress, makeup, and dangling earrings. My hair looked bouncy, with luscious curls. I felt good.

I posted a video on social media in which I explained being stood up, and said that even though I was without a partner, I was taking myself out on a date. I tagged it as: #SexyBrilliant.

I ended up going to a concert in town and having a great time. However, my magical night did not end there.

Can you guess what happened next? I logged into Instagram and saw that a casting agency in Hollywood had watched my #SexyBrilliant video. I had numerous messages from this casting agency, asking me to call them. I initially thought someone was playing a joke on me. I ignored the messages and went to bed on a high note of self-dating and being my own friend.

The next morning, I had an email from the casting agency asking me for an interview. I agreed to the interview. I was curious; this was my first time being scouted through social media. At this point, I was not allowing myself to get too excited about it. I chose to remain aware of how I directed my time, energy, and excitement. I did not want to place unrealistic expectations or hopes on this project. I decided I would proceed with optimistic caution.

Eventually, after weeks and weeks of paperwork and plenty of phone calls to my lawyer, the casting agency and I ended up talking on the phone. During the interview, I was grilled about my dating life. My sex life. My status as a full-time single mother. My life in general. It was a long interview. Two weeks later, I got the news that I had passed that stage of the interview process. I felt like the stars had aligned. I was grateful for this opportunity to share my special brand of sass and my message of radical self-acceptance with the world.

Now I would move to the next stage: another set of interviews with a team in Los Angeles. This process went on for some time. At every step, there were documents and contracts, including non-disclosure agreements and security clearances.

After nine weeks, I got the news that I had made it onto reality television. I made an effort to focus on the present; mindfully, I let my team know that I would be away from work for a few weeks, as work must always go on, even if the boss is out of commission. I knew I was experiencing the consequences of being "too ambitious," and I loved it. Work was so busy—my business was full of everything I dreamed of.

Eventually, after finalizing the paperwork and security clearances, I went to Hollywood. I appeared as myself on a dating television show to find love and my soul mate. I should mention that the idea of finding love on reality television was unusual, exciting, and promising. It was definitely different from my usual playground—online dating.

Again, I proceeded without expectations. I reminded myself that I am more than a media show, a book, a failed date, or a successful business deal. I am a divine beacon of love and light. Everything that goes on around me is what it is. It is not who I am. It is how life is right now. And it will change.

I kept this as my philosophy throughout filming because I knew that, at any moment, life could change again.

Fat, Loud, and Ambitious Hollywood Star

My experience in Hollywood was fun, exciting, and very emotional. The standards were changing, and fat, loud, ambitious women are more acceptable in Hollywood today than they once were. However, the way that diversity in the media is portrayed shows that there is still a long way to go. All people are worthy of love and acceptance, no matter who is watching.

Trusting the process, I have come to believe that every circumstance and person I encounter is my teacher. I trust life, and I believe life will always give me valuable tools. I considered the opportunity to go on a dating show, on Hollywood reality television as a learning experience. It was an opportunity for a new start. Would I meet the person of my dreams there?

I couldn't know the answer to that, unless I made an effort to try it. I only knew that I was one hundred percent ready to give this opportunity the chance it deserved. I jumped into the in-between. In doing so, I opened myself up to more possibilities in romance, partnerships, and new beginnings.

At the end of the day, I am a big, old, softie. I knew that the Hollywood experience would help me grow as a person and teach me more about myself. I was more than excited to access the tools and resources Los Angeles offered, and even though the control freak in me disliked the idea of not being the one to call the shots, I was ready to jump in with all my enthusiasm.

This opportunity came to me as a result of a failed third date with James. Thanks, James for standing me up! He proved my theory that "failures" are in fact amazing opportunities just waiting to happen.

Many may wonder why I went on television to look for love. My answer is, why not? I never expected to have the opportunity to participate in a dating show on reality television. I was hoping for true love—and adventure, fun, sex, and personal growth, too! After years of inner work, I knew myself, and I was happy to be on the show and one hundred percent committed to playing an active role in finding love.

At the time, I was dreaming about a relationship, and it scared me. Love and fear are opposites. To receive love, you have to mindfully leave fear behind. Somewhere deep down, I still felt unworthy of love. The feeling of unworthiness is our emotions talking to us, and emotions are sacred, so it's important to pay attention to them. Being aware of our emotions is what provides us with inner strength and consequently healing. I was acutely aware that I felt afraid of love and relationships. However, I believed that if I did not give myself a chance to possibly meet someone and "rise" in love, I would never know what it was like.

Yes, you read that right. I wanted to rise in love, not fall. I do not believe in falling in love, because falling hurts. Rising in love simply means growing more in love, every day.

Being open to possibility requires taking a risk. On the television show, I might not meet anyone or I could meet someone, the odds were the same. I faced the possibility of being ridiculed. I could be rejected, or many other in-between possibilities.

It was a challenge to accept myself exactly as I was and put myself in the spotlight, knowing I would face criticism, judgement, and hate. I reminded myself: it was my time to shine, in spite of my body size and any other insecurities I might have had. I remember telling myself that insecurity is a powerful enemy.

I am a willing risk-taker and going on reality television was a gamble. I was open to the opportunity of meeting someone new. Often, the anxiety of taking an action or of failing is what stops people from achieving their vision. The fear of failing is also a way for the mind to control you. If you want to achieve your goals, personal or professional, you must take that first step. When you face anxiety, it's important to take the first step regardless.

Slowly, with mindful practice, you will realize the less fearful you are, the younger and more powerful you feel. You connect with your inner child even more, making you feel healthy and more vibrant.

In-Between 2.0

There was a time in my life where I had to choose between a real estate career and writing this, the first book in the Sexy Brilliant™ series. It was a cold winter day in January 2017. I had just finished nine grueling months of real estate school. I sat in my car in a snowstorm, watching the snow fall onto my windows. I was experiencing massive anxiety attacks at that moment. At any second, sweat might have begun pouring out of my armpits. I got a headache just thinking about entering my new real estate office. I was nervous, anxious, and stressed, as my intuition told me I was in-between.

Getting out of the car meant making a major choice. I was following the same path that all my classmates were: signing up to work in real estate. Later, I realized that my unusually sweaty armpits were my body's way of giving me clues that something was really off with my decision.

An inner voice was telling me this was wrong for me. My soul, my instinct, cried out. I was torn because I wanted to keep to the pack mentality and do what everyone else was doing—what *I* was supposed to be doing. My decision was swayed by the potential earnings in the field, and the easy, comfortable choice of following what my friends were doing. As I sat in the car, I asked myself: *Is this really what I want? Am I really going to go back to the corporate world?*

The answer was no. I started the car. I drove away from that office instead of going inside. My sweat disappeared, my headache cleared, and I felt less anxious. At that time, I chose not to tell anyone about my decision to walk away from a potentially lucrative career. I knew I was "weak" and would have been easily persuaded into changing my mind. I made this decision with my heart, not my rational mind, and I felt protective of that choice. I didn't want anyone to attempt to try and talk me out of following my heart.

In retrospect, even though the connection with my divinity was not clear—even if I did not know at the time what I was doing with the Sexy Brilliant™ Foundation and my life purpose—saying no to that office opened many other doors for me. Learning to be comfortable with being in-between entirely changed my life and will change yours too.

Meditations on Being In-Between

I had been having in-between feelings for a while. I felt torn and confused, even before I was faced with choosing between using my real estate degree or writing a book.

One warm Saturday, I was out meditating by the river near the forest and enjoying the sun. I was in pain; emotionally, I was lost. I had my hands full. I was transitioning between work and education, as I was going to college full-time and studying energy work through a mentor-ship program with my guide, Masaki, who encouraged me to find my life purpose. I was learning, once again, that awareness of my purpose does not come easily, but everything I look for outside myself is always already within me.

That afternoon, I was sitting in the sun, as I do during my daily spiritual practice. I observed everything around me, watching the river water flow. It was the middle of the day, my most creative time. Nature was blooming and summer was at its full glory. As I sat gazing into the water, I pondered: *What gifts do I have? What gifts can I share? Why is everything so difficult? What am I born to do? What is my life purpose?*

I recounted everything that I had struggled with: my failures, marriage, divorce, feeling like the black sheep of the family, learning, addiction, depression, and so on. I was always seeking but never finding. What exactly was I born to do? Was my purpose to sell real estate? Was it to walk dogs? Was it to have another arranged marriage? Or was it something bigger than me? In this spiritual place, Sexy Brilliance happened for me.

In spite of my revelation, my self-doubts continued. I had to separate myself from my thoughts. This began to bring me the peace that I needed. After much meditation and contemplation, I surrounded myself with people who were wiser and stronger than me, who could support the work I needed to do. My dating addiction and subsequent cry for help led me to people who assisted me in getting on the path of empowerment.

That day, through immense pain and emotional suffering,

I found my life's purpose. I believe Sexy Brilliance had also been searching for me. From that day, whenever I received a text message from a potential mate asking how I was doing, I replied, "Always sexy, always brilliant." It kind of stuck! Through the years as a single parent, my struggles and my failures became my greatest gift. Imagine that!

In-between takes on a new urgency when addictions, rationalizations, avoidance, frustrations, agreements, and reality all coincide. In-between is not always a choice, and circumstances can cause us to make hard decisions. In-between can sometimes feel like being stuck.

Rebel at Sexy Brilliant

You might think of me as a rebel, but it's truly not intentional. I disrupt, but it is always in service of the highest good. My relationships, obsessive compulsive behaviours, past hurts, and addictive personality have gotten me to where I am today.

For example, shortly after the end of my marriage, I wanted to move to India to raise Anahat. Keeping my daughter close to my family seemed desirable but ultimately would have been destructive to both Anahat and myself.

As the daughter of a single mother in India, my child would not be accepted. Patriarchy does not like people who don't fit into its carefully designed boxes. Being different is a threat to its labels, as they are known to help maintain the illusion of control.

Divorced single mothers, sexually free individuals, and the LGBTQIA+ community fall outside of these boxes. It takes a lot of courage to choose to walk away from those traditional values when doing so can result in shame, isolation, and public censure.

In the end, although it was uncomfortable, I chose to stay in the in-between following my divorce. I remained in Canada.

Dealing with discomfort in the moment saved me a lot of pain in the long run. If I had gone back to India, the outcome would not have been healthy for me or Anahat. In Indian society, the culture is patriarchal. It takes immense inner courage and support to leave a relationship, and due to lack of financial resources, education, and codependency, very few who want to leave are actually able to do so. Women who get divorced need a great deal of courage and strength to deal with the consequences, therefore many women continue to live in abusive marriages. Our culture can be extremely cruel to women who don't toe the patriarchal line, because such women are often perceived as threats to the rest of the society. It takes courage and bravery to choose the in-between in these circumstances. Inner confidence, acceptance, and self-knowledge play a big part in helping women like me survive.

I have been through some tough times in my life. My journey is ongoing, and while it has been fun, it has also been filled with growth, an abundance of emotion, plenty of tears, and a whole lot of self-searching. I have grown since then, but I can positively say I am still on this journey of self-discovery.

When In-Between Becomes Life-Threatening

Sometimes our in-between threatens our very existence and becomes a struggle to survive. A few years ago, in the scariest in-between of my life, my partner Trevor kicked me out of the house. He was an alcoholic who struggled with bipolar disorder and depressive mood swings. In that moment of shame and desperation, when I didn't know where I would go or what I would do, I cried and prayed, prayed and cried. The prayer was a meditation. I kept saying, "I'm sorry." Over and over again, I said the words.

True healing happens when you can forgive yourself for

the grief you have caused in your own life and in the lives of others. Those of us who suffer the shame of relationship abuse or struggle with mental health issues have it harder because shame keeps us isolated and makes it so much more difficult to reach out or find help.

I remember falling asleep in the car, still saying, "I'm sorry, I'm sorry." I said I was sorry to the universe, to all my ancestors, to myself, to my partner, to my family, and to all that I was. I lived in my car for a brief period. I continued to pray. I meditated, rested, and dealt with my tumultuous emotions. It was the only way for me to cope with my circumstances. Because of the unhealthy situation at home, I was afraid to go back. I finally decided that my only choice was to go to a women's shelter, yet I did not go. I didn't utilize the resources at hand because I lacked the courage and self-esteem to reach out to ask for help. I felt shame. I found myself in-between.

Three days later, after living in the car without much food, I finally found the courage to go back home to pick up clothes and money. I still wasn't sure where I was going to go or what I would do next. I had zero cash flow. Everything I had was invested in real estate, the market, or long-term investments. I remember telling myself that things had to change; this couldn't continue for much longer. I didn't have the self-worth or confidence at that time in my life to make the decisions I would make now.

Even though it was dangerous, I ended up staying in the relationship with Trevor for another three months. I wasn't brave enough to let go. I wasn't sure what to expect. We fear to flee what we know in exchange for the unknown. I went back to the same toxic situation, because staying with an alcoholic was better than the shame that yet another broken relationship would bring to me and my family.

When I finally left Trevor for good, I cursed myself for

the lack of awareness that led me to be in this situation. However, once I came to the decision that self-criticism was unhealthy for my mental, emotional, and physical health, I took back my power. I empowered myself to move on. I moved out. I restarted my life. It took great courage to reclaim my power.

I continue to work on myself. Now, I permit myself to stand up and say no to situations that are unhealthy. It took me a long time and a lot of effort and willpower to get here. I am more empowered because of all my experiences and even my addictions. It took me many years to say yes to things that work and no to things that don't. I don't judge myself for my past.

You are who you are because of where you have been and the life you have lived. There is no judgement or need to judge yourself for your learning experiences. I learned to make better decisions based on my past. For example, I now say no to bad sex! I'm kidding. However, the decisions that seem simple are the ones that help you move past being in-between or stuck somewhere you do not want to be.

Activity: Chapter Four

Do you know how to listen to your inner voice? Your intuition? How can you ensure that you are making decisions from your heart's brilliant desires and not from your ego's need for control?

In the following exercise, you will use your intuition as an important and fun tool. The insights you have here will help you benefit from the next few chapters. You will differentiate your mind's voice from your sexy, divine, inner voice during in-between moments.

Circle the "right" answer in each row. Focus on your choice, and remember that you are choosing a personal preference. In this case, the right answer is the first answer that comes to your mind.

Remember, your exercises and answers are private. Choosing black, meditation or Paris doesn't make you a better or worse person than anyone else. Do not judge yourself. Do not compare.

Choose one of the following:

Oral	←	→	Anal
Black	←	→	White
Paris	←	→	New York
New Delhi	←	→	Montreal
Man	←	→	Woman
Meditation	←	→	Alcohol
One Night Stand	←	→	Relationship

Flight	←	→	Drive
Money	←	→	Happiness
Green	←	→	Blue
Threesome	←	→	Monogamy
Big Boobs	←	→	Big Dick
Jazz	←	→	Hip Hop
External Beauty	←	→	Inner Beauty
Obesity	←	→	Anorexia
Stealing	←	→	Miserable
Cats	←	→	Dogs
Fat	←	→	Thin
OCD	←	→	Aging
Children	←	→	Animals
Masturbation	←	→	Meditation

How easy was it to choose one or the other? Did you notice yourself being pulled between the two choices? Can you identify what was pulling you? Did you make each decision with your heart, intuition, or mind?

Did you notice that, as soon as the answer appeared in your mind, a second voice pops up to question your first choice? Always choose the voice that isn't rational, because it's pure and heart-centred. You will hear your heart's voice as you develop a true connection with yourself.

Neither answer is good or bad. It is what it is. Can you accept your answer? If you fight yourself about each of your answers, you are keeping your intuition at arm's length. Keep in mind throughout this journey that your intuition is your best ally.

Some people can't make any choice at all. If that's the case, ask yourself what is holding you back from making a choice.

Perhaps you aren't ready to change or acknowledge your own pattern of being. Perhaps your identity is based on your suffering. Perhaps it is based on your addiction to your pain. That's okay, too. Remember, you are perfect as you are.

Many people are afraid to heal, because their identities are based on the trauma and suffering they have experienced. If you feel stuck, it may be because you have no idea how to change from suffering to being. Sexy brilliance will help you create a new relationship with your being, and empower yourself.

If you get frustrated, that's okay! Take a masturbation break, go pee, or lie down for a nap. There is a list of break-time suggestions in the introduction. Pick one and enjoy! You can come back to this book when you're feeling centred. I love you for being here so far. Thank you.

There is no such thing as a right answer. Stop labelling. Just be. You are good enough in this moment, and your very state is perfection. You are complete and whole as you are. Now you are ready for the next stage of your beautiful and abundant life.

Turn the page, unzip your pants. And go.

Chapter Five: Know

Let's manifest some Sexy Brilliance! The next section will explain how to apply the trademarked K.A.U.R. process to your life, brilliance, and experience. This is the method I use in my spiritual, inner work.

K stands for **K**now. After you know yourself you can grow into the next stage, which is A, for **A**ccept. Acceptance means living in awareness of all of yourself. No part of you is the enemy, but you must know yourself before practicing *radical* self-acceptance towards more self-love. U stands for **U**nveil. Unveil and unlearn what you have come to know and accept about yourself. Just like the letter U, life has its ups and downs. In everything you do in life, you are getting to know, accept, and unveil a new being, while unlearning the past programming. You always have the choice to move up from the valley of the U. Finally, the last letter in the K.A.U.R.™ process is R, which stands for **R**elease.

The next four chapters will all dive deep into one of the K.A.U.R.™ process principles. This chapter is devoted to the first principle, **knowledge**.

What are the things you must know? What's important to you? What is your culture or country of origin? How do you label people or things? What are the labels that you most identify with? How do you label yourself? Do you see yourself as only one thing, or many—a mother, wife, woman, and child of the Divine? Are there labels that you use on yourself that deprive you of fully experiencing being human?

Ask yourself the question, "Who am I?" What response comes up first? Your status? Nationality? Gender? Now, ask yourself how these things define you.

Ask again. Who are you deep down? Authentically? Are you lost for answers? Or does this process of knowing come easily for you?

I am innately curious, observe from the conversations around me, and learn from everyone around me. Often, when I interview people for research, I ask a very simple question: "How would you describe yourself, as you are right now, in three words?"

Many people are unable to complete this simple exercise. Most people have no clue what their role is in this world. Each label seems to make it more complicated. Without self-knowledge, self-examination only creates confusion. Self-study is hard but it's the original sexy.

One evening, on a very hot summer day, I was enjoying the outdoor Jazz Festival in Montreal. It's one of the biggest events of its kind in North America. While enjoying the music and my picnic dinner, a tall, somewhat lanky man came and sat next to me. I instantly said hello and complimented him on his attractive shirt. His name was Stuart. Through the evening, we got to know each other as friendly neighbours, sitting side by side, sharing music and an outdoor concert. At the end of our evening, we parted ways, but before I went my way, I asked Stuart to give me three words to describe himself.

Stuart was taken aback and asked me if this was a dating question. I laughed and said no. I told him I was in the process of finishing my first book in the Sexy Brilliant™ series, and I was in the self-development world. Stuart was able to give me only one of the three words. He used the word "different."

I asked him why he considered himself different, and he explained that he didn't watch the news or read newspapers: that made him different. I loved his answer. Self-awareness is the first step toward self-knowledge.

As I have mentioned previously, I am an extrovert, so

it was very easy for me to present my real self during my interaction with Stuart. Ask yourself who you are? What are your strengths, skills, and talents? Again, it comes down to how well you know your authentic self and the purpose of your life. Sometimes you must ask yourself challenging questions to get to the heart of your gifts.

Instead of asking yourself what you want out of life, ask what life wants out of you. You can identify your gifts by asking, What are my abilities, my passions, my purpose? My weaknesses? Until you can answer these simple questions, you will find it's almost impossible to find contentment and happiness. Although, once you have answered them, through the process of transformation, you will begin to feel peace and self-love. You will have worked through the K.A.U.R.™ process and you can experience release.

The Sexy Brilliant philosophy teaches how to work through layers and layers of self-searching to know yourself, inside and out. Feeling *sexy* is empowering, and it comes from who you truly are deep down. Being *brilliant* is exploring all the possibilities with which life has gifted you. Not doing so is a living death sentence. I offer as sad examples the deaths of three famous people who seemed to have it all figured out: Kate Spade, Anthony Bourdain, and Robin Williams. From the outside, it was easy to make assumptions about their happiness based on their celebrity status and commercial success. They seemed like examples of lives well-lived, yet all three chose to commit suicide in the end. I believe their decision came from having long denied a part of themselves they were no longer able to reach and heal. The pain was too great to try to continue through this maze of life any further. May they rest in peace.

I know myself well enough to own that I also struggle with depression and have a manic-depressive personality. However, this is only true in my human form. Depression doesn't exist in the spiritual world. What helps me is to be mindful of all my emotions. Whenever I go through a dark phase in my life, I practice constant awareness of my emotions. I repeat positive, loving messages to *myself*: I am not my business failure. I am not my cancelled date. I am not my fat body. Instead of focusing on what's bringing me down, I repeat that I'm a beacon of love and light. I am in this human form to experience life, and to find and share my purpose of being Sexy Brilliant.

Get to know yourself as an observer of all your emotions. I share myself openly because I want you to feel empowered to know yourself and live life to your full purpose and potential.

The letter K is a symbol for some of the choices you will face in life. The first part of the letter is standing tall. The rest is going in two different directions, up and down, diagonally, just like most of the paradoxes of life.

The better you know yourself, the more likely you are to succeed in the things that you are called to do in this life. Knowing and loving every inch of yourself is the key to being a healthier, happier, and more courageous person. Even though I still have fears, I also have a smile and a steady gaze aimed ahead of me. I can be happy that I didn't let cold logic get in the way of my dreams.

Knowing yourself makes you less afraid of following your inner power. Have faith that it will always lead you to further happiness.

What Do You Dream?

When you live out your dreams, you become responsible for your own joy and happiness. You begin to create paths for more bliss to flow. When you take responsibility for your own joy, it has a powerful ripple effect on others and everything in the world. You then learn to live life on purpose. You follow your dreams and go after your calling, even when it seems to defy all reason.

Dreaming sounds so easy, but it can be challenging. At other times, it doesn't seem difficult at all. When you daydream, fantasize, or visualize your highest good, you allow yourself to be solely guided by your own perfect intuition. You simply must learn to be.

You can practice accepting that everything is perfect just as it is—even during the times when your dreams bring challenges.

Anahat: My Firstborn

Parenting is hard, and single parenting is even harder. Children don't come with an operation manual. Most of the time, parents are winging it—most parents will never admit this, but it's so true. As a full-time, single parent, my goal is to be as brilliant a mom as my daughter is a brilliant child. I have learned so much from her. She has taught me that everything does not have to be perfect for us to share happiness. In fact, we spend a lot of time giggling, finding joy in whatever splendid little events pop up each day.

When it comes to knowing, children are my biggest teachers. Last year, in the middle of nonstop snowstorms, on a day when the temperature was below zero, I suggested to Anahat that we go to Cuba for a holiday.

Anahat rolled her eyes at me and said, "No, Mummy. You need to save up all our money so you can rescue more cats and dogs."

I didn't know how to respond, but at that moment, I was very proud of her. She not only taught me an important lesson about prioritizing, but also reminded me that escapism is not the solution to my issues—including the weather.

When you look at life as one big learning experience, parenting is just another class in the school of life. Even though parents have more life experience than the little beings who share your home, your life, and your womb, you still have so much to learn from them. Every day.

Thanks to my daughter, I have learned to be patient. It is a quality that is considered feminine, which I am able to recognize that I was lacking. For example, in second grade, Anahat decided that she no longer wanted to go to school. Mornings became a nightmare. I had to take a break from parenting and give in to her demands of being a child. It turned out that my seven-year-old was feeling insecure about leaving me, her favourite person in the world, to go to school. Slowly, caring, lovingly, I worked through the emotions of a young child, with the help of a professional.

Asking for help is part of parenting, and it's just as important in asking for help with anything else in life that needs extra love and attention. Every day, as a parent and as an individual, I have an opportunity to work on my personal development.

How is it possible to love a mini version of myself even more than I love myself? Before Anahat arrived, I didn't know how to answer this question. But I do now! I never expected to cancel dates, re-arrange business meetings, and forgo coffee with friends so I could walk my daughter home from school or volunteer with her scout troop. Parenting always lets me surprise myself and do things out of my comfort zone. For example, I had never been camping before, but Anahat and I went together with her friends and their parents.

I discovered that I love being there for my daughter. I love giving my time and energy to things that are important to her. Volunteering, called "*seva*" in the Punjabi language, has always been a big part of my grandparents' legacy. I remember volunteering with them and cooking meals. Seva can take many forms, such as giving time, sending money, donating blood, and so much more. Ultimately, volunteering makes me appreciate and be grateful for what I already have.

If you're feeling depressed or low, consider volunteering—

it can be as simple as walking the neighbour's dog or helping an old person at the grocery store.

Now I volunteer on a regular basis. I fill my home with pets and my daughter's friends, and I feel fulfilled in a way I never experienced before. I now know this kind of joy. For me, helping is part of me knowing myself.

Self-Regulation through Knowing

Dating as a single parent can have challenges that are different from dating when you don't have children. Last week, one of the mothers in my book club told me that she heard that another single mother left her eight-year-old daughter alone overnight in order to spend the night at a boyfriend's house. I was shocked to hear this story. I cannot begin to tell you how much it upset me.

I put myself in the other mother's shoes. Would I ever leave my daughter alone overnight to spend the night at my partner's house? No.

I was able to get centred, calm down, and remind myself that my child would always be my number one priority. In fact, any partner who could possibly encourage leaving a child all alone overnight is irresponsible and selfish: not the kind of person I would want to be with. I had to make an effort to be empathetic to this other mother, who I know through several degrees of separation.

Most people don't set out to be full-time single parents. I surely did not. I certainly didn't obey all the advice in every parenting book either. I know that I don't always do things that will work for everyone, but being ambitious and wanting more, I managed to figure out a way to date, run a business, raise an incredible child, and live a life of bliss. Self-knowledge helps me to balance all of this.

My journey has not been conventional but being a mother

has been an amazing opportunity to learn and grow, both for me and my very patient daughter.

Who Is Number One?

Being a responsible parent also means putting my child first. She is my priority, always. Any potential date, or even a friend, who's worthy of my time will know it and appreciate this part of my life.

Often, I have made a conscious choice to be with family in lieu of working, dating, and meeting people. There was a time when not knowing myself caused me to cultivate relationships to fill an inner void. Without knowing myself, my gifts, or my talents, I wasn't able to accept and consequently love myself. I looked for love, validation, and acceptance outside of myself and outside of my own divinity. My way was to seek out a new relationship after my arranged marriage ended and to look for a man to save me. Rebellious in dating and in my marriage, I thought I could empower myself through another person, by creating connections only with people I wanted to have a romantic relationship with.

Can you imagine the pressure we put on ourselves and on the men we expect to save us?

Very quickly, I realized that I didn't need a romantic connection with someone in order to have an orgasm with them. Until I was face-to-face with the new, real me, I truly believed that my identity was based on having a conventional man-woman relationship, just like my parents and all the other members of my family. I was so desperate to fit in and not be an outcast, and this led me to search for my next relationship.

Some of the men I met online and made connections with included seeking out sex and intimacy. This was my way of escaping from my culture, where I was taught that sex is a part of marriage: women are not meant to enjoy sex. Now I know better; now I know myself and my needs.

I am so grateful to have discovered other ways to connect with my family. I learned that I can still have them in my life, while cultivating my own happiness and peace outside of the narrow confines of their culture.

At Anahat's request, I'm learning to be a stricter parent. One day, we were walking back home from visiting some friends when Anahat turned toward me and asked, "Mummy, why can you not be like other parents and be stricter with me?"

It made me laugh out loud. Truly, out of the mouths of our children! Her innocent questioning often makes me rethink my spiritual parenting methods. Having a predictable routine to follow is important for children. Mornings always begin the same way at our home. Over the course of the week, we do certain activities on the same days of the week. Writing it all down on the calendar keeps us on track. When the inevitable requests for afterschool playdates come around, I point at the calendar. If there's an open square, it is a yes. If it's karate night, it is a no.

What works for one family will not necessarily work for another. Every individual is unique, so it's important to prioritize your needs and come up with a routine and system that work for you and your family.

Indulging Your Inner Child

Parenting is a great tool to help you evolve. It is a way to know yourself, as you take care of your children.

Being surrounded by mother figures somewhere in each of our lives, we know that mothers are all dedicated to this life purpose, but what about the mothering we must give to ourselves? How do we do this? As already discussed in Chapter 3, you can learn to distinguish between your ego and your inner child. I do this by giving my ego a task and giving my inner child my love, just as I give love to my own child.

I have heard some critics say that the ego and the inner child are one and the same. But are they? Not in my life. My inner child wants to play, laugh, and party *all* the time. As I shared earlier, my ego, Claudia, wants to create drama and instill fear. She is also super ambitious. The key to balancing these parts is to live in awareness of all parts of myself. Balance helps me to gain inner confidence, which is also called self-mastery.

Through mastery, you can know, accept, and love all parts of yourself, including your ego and your inner child. For me, this has taken a lot of self-searching and experimentation. I spent so much of my life letting others dictate how I should behave, what I should wear, what I should eat, and even what I should like or dislike. When I set out on my journey of empowerment, it took time to discover what I—me, myself—loved most!

How did I do it? I watched my daughter. I was inspired by how effortlessly she knew that she wanted to take ballet but didn't like badminton. She refused to eat certain foods. She has a mind of her own! She says she loves me, no matter what I wear. She tells me all the time that I am the best mother in the world, right after telling me that she hates me. She makes me laugh at the most inappropriate times. She is my best teacher because she's uninhibited and full of joy. This is what I have learned: children live an easy, simple, and authentic life, free of judgement. We have so much to learn from them.

Moving beyond the criticism of others and living your best life helps keep your inner child alive. Children live in a world where they are freely able to be themselves. They only become inauthentic from experience, as they grow up in a culture and in environments that tell them who they should be rather than encouraging *who they are*. Even if you don't have children yourself, you can remember this: you were a child before you became an adult. Right?

Today and every day, you can accept and live with that in mind. Today and every day, you can keep your inner child alive. You can do things that give you childlike joy again. You are a spiritual being having a human experience. In the spiritual world, age does not exist. You can do things that make you feel young again: dance, sing, eat, and even walk without shoes on.

Going Barefoot

There is pleasure in being, for me. *Being* is such a sexy word. One of the ways I experience pleasure is by grounding myself and walking barefoot. This activity gives me a way to stay balanced and mindful of my mental, physical, emotional, and spiritual health. I walk barefoot whenever the weather permits.

I know myself, and I know my weaknesses; it's very easy for me to lose my balance. Through years of self-work and personal development, I've realized that the closer I am connected to nature, the happier I am. This is where I get to *be*. I connect and find my equanimity.

However, there are rules to going barefoot. Shoes are important for safety and, often, comfort. But when you look at dogs, you see that they walk on their paws and seem to enjoy walking without shoes, so why can I not do the same? I am not saying that shoes are not important, but it feels so much better to be free. When I leave my shoes off, I celebrate myself as beautiful, grounded, and eccentric. Barefoot, I experience life just the way I am. I consider myself to be a child of nature. However, my podiatrist, who is trained in western medicine, does not approve of it. I believe it's healthy to nurture my relationship with the earth, so that I can be one with nature.

Beyond walking barefoot, there are more things you can do to connect to your inner child. Perhaps you can indulge in a movie that made you happy, and gave you the belly laughs of being a child. If you're single, you can spend some time, and even date, partners who are significantly younger than yourself—of a legal age, of course.

Spending time with people younger or older than you is a great experience to have. Think of it as an experiment. You can people-watch. Whether or not you consider yourself artistic, you can even draw the people you observe. As creative humans, you can imagine them as characters from your favourite comic book. You can even imagine what they look like naked!

Connecting with my body connects me to my inner child. Dancing to music on the radio makes me feel young and fun again. I'm not a singer, but I sing loud and proud. I have always found joy in making a fool of myself, especially as a child. Singing is a fun activity to do alone or with friends, in the shower or even outside.

Some other things I practice in an effort to be mindful of the inner child in me include sharing a smile with a baby. This is one of the best things you can do to make yourself young again and keep your inner child alive. You can even indulge in giggles with them. Often, when I hear my daughter giggle, I also laugh nonstop. Her little sounds of laughter are like music to my ears.

Observe children. I may be stressed, exhausted, and busy, but when I need a cheer-up, I watch children walking, playing in the snow, climbing a tree, and just being in the moment. That, to me, is how I can keep my inner child alive. Watch children be children, and learn how to bring some of their natural exuberance into your own life.

As a child, I was "too loud," and I never quite fit in. As an adult, I connected with myself, got to know myself, and recognized that being too loud is actually my gift. My childlike nature was part of my authentic self. What others saw as my weakness was actually my brilliance.

The H-Factor

As I have mentioned, there was a time in my life when I was addicted to dating. On my dating profile, I said "I have the H-Factor going." Mentioning my H-Factor was always a great opener for conversations. The H-Factor means I am *happy, hungry, horny* and sometimes *humble*!

I remember having conversation after conversation on different dating apps. Whenever I was chatting with more than two to three men on dating sites, I would just copy and paste my explanation about what "H-Factor" means. The H-Factor was one of the most fun things I ever experimented with. A lot of times, men would laugh and want to know more. Some would be too shocked to continue chatting. A few times, as soon as I shared about the H-Factor, I would get unmatched!

I know that mentioning my needs and desires up front could seem "too loud," but I know myself. The H-Factor breaks down my *raison d'être* and explains it clearly. For example, my goal is to be *happy*: the happiest person I know.

I am also always *hungry*; I will eat something, and a few minutes later, I'm hungry for food again. Sigh!

As for the third part of the H-Factor, I am always *horny*. My sexual energy is high, just like the rest of my energy, including my spiritual energy.

And yes, I am sometimes *humble*—although, the other day Anahat told me that I should stop kidding myself, because I am never humble. In all honesty, the H-Factor constantly changes and evolves, just like life. I am proud of knowing and sharing all of myself with you. It does take courage to be loud and flamboyant.

Being "too loud" allows me to be daring and bold, to take risks.

What are the qualities that you were ashamed of as a child? How do those qualities help you live your best life now? How have you adapted to accept those things in yourself and use them to serve the highest good?

Receiving Compliments

Last week I was in a business meeting with my Mr. T, an alias for someone very well known in the film industry. We were discussing my upcoming projects, including my new radio show. Mr. T. was very kind and gave me a compliment about my ambitious personality. It was so unexpected to receive a real compliment from a complete stranger that I was completely dumbfounded. I didn't know how to react to a genuine and sincere compliment, even though I give them all the time.

Since my experience with Mr. T., I've been thinking about giving and receiving compliments with grace. Now, I am on a mindful mission to welcome compliments.

Overachievers know what I'm talking about. Because my standards are so high, I find it impossible to be graceful about my success. I know my shortcomings, and I know my strengths. Being a full-time student of life, this is something I want to change about myself. I would like to learn to take a compliment which is a bit of a challenge for me. However, awareness of a situation is the first step toward changing it—right?

Knowing yourself as you currently are allows you to shift forward in the K.A.U.R.™ process, toward acceptance. I encourage you to know yourself in this beautiful perfect state that you are already in. I encourage you to give out genuine compliments. Be mindful. Personal self-work is ongoing and non-stop. Consistent dedication to all of the Sexy Brilliant processes supports you where your best transformations happen.

Activity: Chapter Five

Mirror, mirror on the wall ... who's the Sexiest, most Brilliant Inner Divinity of all?

And just look back at that beautiful reflection staring back at you. **Mirror Therapy** is a tool that I use daily... many, many times a day, if necessary!

Get in front of a mirror. If you have a body image complex, get in front of a full-body mirror. Naked. Good. Now pucker up and give that sweet reflection a wet one. Declare what you see every day. Our perceptions change as we have ups and downs. What matters is that we always go back to the mirror to admire that SB soul.

I dare you to take the 30-day Mirror Therapy challenge! At least once a day, you will stand in front of the mirror for several minutes (or longer) and stare with love. Optional: Masturbate at the same time. ;) You'll be amazed with how your perception changes from day 1 to 30.

1	2	3	4	5	6	7
8	9	10	11	12	13	14
15	16	17	18	19	20	21
22	23	24	25	26	27	28
29	30	30-day Mirror Therapy challenge!				

Bite Your Tongue! As you practice Mirror Therapy, you may catch yourself saying (or thinking) some pretty nasty things. Acknowledge them, without giving them any more attention than that.

Every thought is a passing one, good or bad. The goal is to have more of the good than the bad. So, how to do this?

By using **Sexy Brilliant Vocabulary** at all times. Careful with the words you choose to recite back to yourself. Words matter, and your subconscious mind will register any negative words and will create more of the same s**t. If you're depressed, refuse to use the "d" word. If you're scared, you will say that you are fearless.

In your 30-day calendar, use a red pen to write the word that came to mind, but that you chose not to say because they were self-limiting. Remind yourself (with lots of compassion) that it is OK to have these negative thoughts. They are passing, just like everything else. Acknowledge them and move on!

** *Hint: If, over the course of the month, you start to notice fewer and fewer negative thoughts pop up, then you know it's already taking effect!*

** *For those of you who are still getting many negative thoughts, don't worry—you just haven't fully integrated this yet. Did you know that habits take 90 days (on average) to form? Guess what? Your next step is to continue this exercise for a total of 90 days!*

Seeing is believing! Just as powerful as Mirror Therapy is

Photo-Therapy.

Self-portraits (dressed or naked) are the ultimate way to begin accepting your SB self. At first, you may feel shy or silly. But with time, you will start to strike that perfect pose and flash that brilliant smile. You will know how to stand to get the "best version" of yourself. You will laugh into the camera and instantly feel happier. You will literally watch your confidence grow.

I strongly encourage experimenting with Photo-Therapy at different times of the day. Monitor and see if you can detect patterns that work in your favour. Ask yourself what makes it so brilliant?

DAY 1	DAY 2	DAY 3
Time _____	Time _____	Time _____
AM / PM	AM / PM	AM / PM
_____	_____	_____
Fav Pic	Fav Pic	Fav Pic
_____	_____	_____
What makes it SB?	What makes it SB?	What makes it SB?

Chapter Six: Accept

In Chapter Five, I shared my insights about self-knowledge. This is the first step toward becoming a sexier version of yourself. In the next step of the K.A.U.R.™ process, you will learn about acceptance.

Self-acceptance comes from accepting yourself in your current, beautiful state. There is no self-acceptance without the awareness that self-knowledge brings. When you don't accept yourself, you don't know yourself. Acceptance puts you in touch with your own Sexy Brilliance. Let me rephrase that: RADICAL self-acceptance is what is needed to become a Sexy Brilliant star.

One major barrier that many people face is difficulty accepting that they are meant for greatness. It's so easy to get distracted by external messages of worth that constantly tell us that we aren't good enough, we are never enough, and that we must change ourselves to be accepted and liked by others in order to fit in. All over the world, in both Eastern and Western culture, emotions are used as a tool that others can exploit. Emotions are commercialized. Businesses take advantage of your insecurities and oversell you products which they insist will improve your health, appearance, life, perceived social status, worthiness, and, in turn, promising happiness they cannot deliver.

Don't let the world keep you hidden from discovering your divine genuine self. Instead, follow your heart. Absolutely nothing else matters. As long as you aren't harming anyone in your search for personal development and inner wealth, do whatever is needed to give yourself the life that you want.

Perhaps, like me, you have dimmed your light because it scares you. In my experience, when you shine to your full potential, you will be judged and rejected because you are so powerful. You haven't been ready to fully experience your Sexy Brilliance. Dimming your sexiness makes you feel socially acceptable. You sacrifice your potential so that you fit in.

It takes a lot of courage to love yourself and shine fully. Inside, your unconscious whispers, You are not courageous enough. Self-doubt is always walking one step behind confidence. Inner confidence grows exponentially when you start accepting the brilliance inside of you. Furthermore, self-confidence comes from not tolerating judgement or lack of respect from yourself or others. You've been violent toward yourself all your life by not accepting yourself.

In my case, I have spent my life resisting the choices imposed upon me. From an arranged marriage and unrealistic expectations to being a single mom, I have struggled with lacking confidence, desiring affection, and needing to make money. Only when I accepted myself and stopped resisting, could I walk in step with the scheme and beauty of life. With self-acceptance, I can flow with life. When I accepted, I truly started to open my wings.

What You Allow Will Continue

Saying no and building self-respect does not come naturally for some people. Many are programmed, encultured, and unknowingly living in self-loathing, even as they try to do their best. It's nearly impossible to break free without the spiritual and self-empowerment tools of self-awareness and courage.

For example, I was in a long-distance relationship with Shane. We often used text messages to communicate, as we were both on different continents at that time. Shane asked me to send him naked pictures of myself. I laughed and told him that I don't send naked pictures.

My decision to say no really upset Shane. He was upset that I didn't trust him. I reassured Shane that it wasn't because I didn't trust him. I was just uncomfortable sending naked pictures of myself.

Shane and I ended up breaking up over this. As you can imagine, this break-up really upset me, and I mourned this loss; however, I was true to myself. I talked about this break-up with my therapist. She helped me realize that by saying no to naked pictures I had actually accepted and empowered myself and my truth.

Beating yourself up and allowing others to do the same to you is not okay. Saying no when your sixth sense is guiding you is a perfectly acceptable choice. In my case, my choice led to more self-respect.

Perhaps, like me, you also have a Shane in your life? With true acceptance of yourself—once you know yourself—the first thing to accept is that love and relationships should never hurt.

Respect should never be an option. Just like saying no to Shane, I have been setting boundaries and teaching others how to treat me. Whatever happens in my life is the outer reaction of my inner world. That's why, the more you envy others, the less you actually possess. The more you hate, the more you are hated. The happier you are, the happier life becomes. Just like the Law of Attraction, we attract the energy that we give out.

When you accept yourself completely, you can decide what to transform. Your whole life changes. What, in your life, are you still resisting? What have you not accepted? Who are you angry at and what is holding you back?

So often, people blame others for the fact that things didn't work out the way they wanted. I challenge you to accept that you can turn even these challenging, frustrating experiences into lessons that help you accept what you are and truly evolve into something brilliant and beautiful.

The power is yours.

Rejection and Living in Love with Your Ego

I have always wanted lots of children and a big, big family. You know—so there is more love around. A few years ago, I asked a good friend Ali to consider having children with me. I also asked him to marry me—but I will share those juicy details another time.

After a substantial amount of careful consideration, Ali said no to children. He didn't want children in his life. He was kind, straightforward, and calm about his decision. Yes, it was a refusal, but I chose not to look at it as rejection. I used this experience as an opportunity to dig deeper within myself.

In fact, Ali's refusal was not really a rejection, because it empowered me. This experience taught me an important lesson about not taking rejection personally. I was able to walk away with my ego, or sense of self, intact. Everyone has an ego; it can be considered your essential sense of self, or your idea of who you think you are. Being rejected is seldom easy, whether it's for personal or professional reasons. Simply being aware of your ego and even becoming friends with it can help you see how your ego creates dis-empowerment in your life. Getting to know, befriend, and love your ego is also part of the process of acceptance and becoming a sexier version of yourself.

The good news is that Ali and I are still good friends. His rejection was not personal, because he chose the best decision for himself. However, I am still looking for a new baby daddy, so if you know someone suitable, please do send them my way!

Whether you are already in a relationship or thinking of getting into the dating scene, it's critical to be in the right place—physically, emotionally, spiritually, sexually, and mentally.

You should venture out on your dating escapades feeling like the sexy person you really are. Sexy Brilliance can be applied in every area, especially when you're putting yourself out there in new and scary situations, including career changes.

When you know and accept yourself, it matters less and less what other people think. You will live less and less with a fear energy. By holding on to other people's rejections, you create resentment and anger, which in turn lowers your vibration and creates blocks in your journey towards self-actualization.

Every time you get into an angry or hurtful situation—or even a pleasant one—with another being, your energies can get tangled up. Unless you consciously untangle yourself by practicing forgiveness, you can get stuck in a very complex web of negativity. In those situations, rejection will only contribute to your self-doubt. Let go of old hurt and emotions that no longer serve you. Stop dwelling on the past and give yourself the gift that is the present moment; we have the power to choose a new beginning when we live mindfully in the *now*.

Here are some of my favourite ways to increase confidence and get into the right frame of mind to live fearlessly.

Accepting What Is

You shouldn't feel guilty because you want to move to another country, have a better life, feel beautiful, want a one-night sexual encounter, or enjoy abundance. Unfortunately, some people mock those desires. Society uses shame to make it seem unhealthy to want to have more. It creates confining, man-made boundaries.

Anyone who is ambitious is labelled as "egotistical" or "greedy." The lesson is that everyone should be content with the bare minimum: having a roof over your head and a job that pays the bills. As you learn to defy your past experiences and stand up for your voracious self, you will feel like a rebel much of the time. Religion, politics, culture, and the collective ego will oppose you. Do not let that stop you from being your genuine self.

Your ego may act out and speak up at interesting times. As I was writing this book, I met a new man. His name was Daniel. He was a tall, French-Canadian man in his mid-thirties, and very beautiful. Daniel and I had been trying to go out for a long time; however, the stars never aligned, as our schedules just never seemed to match.

Finally, we made plans to meet one weekend. In the days leading up to our date, we continued to share communication. When the weekend arrived, after a lot of self-knowledge and self-acceptance of what is a priority in my life, I messaged Daniel and said, "I know we have never met, and please do not take it the wrong way, but I would rather have a sex date than a dinner date. Is that something that is possible tonight?"

Daniel very politely declined for his own personal reasons: he was looking for a relationship. My main focus at that time was not to start a new relationship, but to finish the consuming project of writing and publishing my book. My work overtook all other aspects of my life. I accept that I have evolved since then and have definitely changed. Now, I acknowledge that sex is sometimes just the pleasurable release I need. Emotions, such as love and affinity, come with a lot of time. I could not spend my energy and time romancing Daniel, because that did not match my focus at the time.

Instead of running after Daniel, or leading him on, I accepted my sexual needs. That's what allowed me to speak with honesty and avoid wasting our time.

I attribute this acceptance to allowing Claudia, my ego, to have her say.

Claudia is also constantly encouraging me to live my dreams. Having a healthy relationship with my ego has helped me to grow as a person. Initially, when I started to write this book, she was always trying to stop me. Instead of resisting her, I constantly gave her love, gratitude, and a place in my life. I am gently learning to walk hand-in-hand with her to follow a more authentic path. It might not be the path my old, outdated self might choose, but thanks to my new love—myself—I am aware of life.

With Daniel, I knew and accepted that I had other priorities than a relationship. This is one way of knowing, accepting, and being aware of all my feelings; it's how I have learned to manage my emotions. In the past, because I didn't know how to handle my emotions, myself, and my needs, I gave away my power to men, addictions, and relationships—to name just a few of the distractions.

I am unveiling my deepest, intimate life to empower you to connect more to yourself and accept all your emotions. You never need to dim your light to get what you desire.

Yin and Yang

Ego exists! The ego is a mind pattern that influences your decisions. The ego is what gives you ambition, self-protection, and the ability to present a strong image, among other things. To live a balanced life, you need a healthy ego.

However, an outdated ego creates drama, threatens, cheats, hurts, fears, evokes bad memories, and causes pain. What can I say about my ego? Truthfully, Claudia loves drama. She thrives on drama. Ha! Most of us don't realize how our egos get us into trouble and tricky situations.

When you learn to dance with your "dark side," you will see how your good and bad are like yin and yang. You have that duality within you. It's important to love both sides in order to maintain a balance. That's perhaps the best gift you can give yourself in this lifetime. The point to keep in mind is that the dark isn't negative or a bad thing to have. The simple comparison of night and day comes to mind. Because there is night, which is usually quiet and calm and often associated with femininity, you can truly appreciate the sun, and the bright fire it projects.

In other words, the dark is needed to help balance out the light. In my own journey of self-acceptance, I have learned to embrace the parts of me that I do not always love. And this notion that ego is bad? Of course it arises, in large part due to our cultural and societal reasoning. An important mantra that I tell myself is: never be scared of your dark side.

You can choose not to live in dread of your dark side or you can choose to accept all parts of yourself. Through sharing my own successes, failures, and life situations, I am able to give my creative side a voice. Unveiling into who I am now takes away its ability to control my life, and I release the embarrassment of my past. Why should I deny my darkness, my negative feelings, or my ego? The fear that darkness is negative and that the ego is bad is what keeps many people from empowering themselves.

Accepting All Emotions

Learning to accept the full range of your emotions brings new understanding. Like many people, you were probably not taught how to manage the difficult emotions, such as worry, heartache, anger, guilt, and depression. Most people use two mechanisms to handle these negative emotions: either attempting to flee or escape from harmful feelings or over-thinking them. In psychology this is known as the "fight or flight response."

Let's exercise a new habit around this dichotomy. How about accepting these difficult emotions, living through them, being one with them, and letting them go? Instead of allowing emotions to be filtered through your ego, which creates drama, can you embrace them and love them into something better?

I self-talk my way out of dramatic situations by making Claudia feel validated. I tell Claudia: "I love you. We are together, now and forever." It does calm her down.

Learning to dance with my ego this way, with joy, kindness, and humour, allows less sabotage from the ego. Even when there's a deliberate attempt from the ego to deal damage, you'll be aware of it. The joy of being aware of yourself and living a rich life will allow you to embrace this duality. Let me be clear: the ego is not a negative construct in itself, but minimizing the ego's role is vital to shining in your sexiness, happiness, and self-care. The mind is an important part of what makes you who you are.

Unfortunately, as I have learned with Claudia's help, when my ego isn't healthy and I have a poor sense of myself, I can be stubborn and often hurt myself and others.

The thing is, when you shine to your full potential, you'll be judged very harshly and rejected. All of a sudden, through your own personal development and consequent transformation, you are seen as a very powerful star. In the past, dimming my loudness, my ambitiousness, and my sexiness has made me socially acceptable and allowed me to fit in. It does take a lot of courage, strength, and a certain bravery to know, accept, and love myself and fully shine.

When you don't know yourself, your ego keeps whispering to you that you are not enough. This only adds to your self-doubt. Inner confidence comes from accepting your light and your dark. Even though we're committed to our own growth work and sexy journey, we must still accept that most people around us are unwilling to go on our journey. You can't change them or save them. Yet, you have to accept them in a non-judgemental way. You have to set boundaries and create limits, to make sure that their rejection never becomes toxic. Never allow others to lower your frequency.

The simple habit of gratitude can transform all our relationships. I have two dogs and one cat: Lianel, Baby, and Billu (née Auggie). One of the things I practice on a daily basis is to say thank you to my dog Lianel for choosing me. All my animals get to hear "thank you" at least five times a day. I know, how crazy is that?

This habit started about seven years ago, when I was getting over yet another heartbreak. This time, a boyfriend who dumped me for my cousin. I was massively depressed. Part of me was angry, hurt, and broken; yet, I was thankful to be alive. I needed to connect with divine love and energy. Instead of going out to pray, meditate, or practice religion, I chose to look at the energy that lived next to me. At that time, it was only me and my one-year-old dog Lianel, a black poodle mix.

I said, "Thank you, Lianel for choosing me as your mommy."

Lianel looked at me and his eyes smiled, as if he understood what I had said. Yes, it's only one-way communication, but this "pet therapy" helped me heal. Lianel's presence and his unconditional love soothed and comforted me. The more I thanked him, the more I was able to accept and mourn the betrayal of my loved ones—in this case my own cousin, who was always more than a sister. I did this without fighting my emotions and I was able to accept my sadness.

Slowly, practising constant gratitude in acts as simple as being thankful to Lianel, I started transforming my sadness, betrayal, and depressive emotions into thankfulness. I realized that I had been able to trick my mind. I said to myself, "How lucky are you that you found out about this betrayal?"

The more I said it, the more I believed I was the luckiest girl in the world, and the more grateful I became. The more thankful I became, the more reasons I found to send sexy, positive vibes to myself and those around me. My goodness came back to me tenfold.

You can live a life of action and gratefulness, too. Now, my instinct tells me that sharing this story is okay. Perhaps it will help you find your way of expressing your truth. Part of me feels very fearful in sharing this story because of how eccentric I could seem and be perceived. Who thanks their dog? Moreover, who names their dog Lianel? I have never ever spoken about this betrayal or heartbreak, you are the first person to know my dark secret. It's a bit scary to be so open and honest, but when I accept my intimate side and unveil myself as I am, I understand my own power. Magic begins to happen.

In writing this particular story, I allow myself to be guided by my divine sexy voice. You can listen to your inner voice, too. While it's important to seek out different opinions, it's even more important to trust your own voice. Cultivate the courage to use your sexy inner voice. The more you listen to your inner voice, the stronger it gets.

Try it. This way, you come closer to getting to know yourself, your own gifts, and the vast possibilities that are in front of you. You can ask yourself what will make you feel good, and then follow through in action. You can then ask yourself if you could have done something to have a better result.

Accepting the Past

If you talk negatively to yourself, perhaps you're letting your doubts run the show. If so, then you have been self-harming all your life. It's time to change that. The moment you become aware of your ego, you win. It's that simple.

Your mind will constantly try to bring you back to the past and distract you from the present moment, the *now-ness*, but as soon as you practice a heightened state of awareness, you will be able to dance with your ego and to even make fun of yourself and enjoy the process of transformation.

Awareness comes from radical self-acceptance and knowledge of the self from within, and your journey through life is incredibly unique. Life is a gift, and who you are today is a result of what has happened to you in the past. There are never any mistakes. Everything is a learning experience and exactly as it should be. Every part of the past is a gift, if you choose to look at it like that.

Self-Worth and How to Create It

The funny thing is, when you rise in love with yourself, everyone and everything around you looks beautiful. You attract even more love into your life. Another part of choosing to live in love by accepting yourself means practising self-love. It's incredibly challenging to maintain your self-love when you don't know our own worth. Not only can you know your worth, but you can also consciously create it.

My self-worth was revealed in my earlier example of my conversation with Daniel, the guy I had asked a sex date. I chose to say yes to sex on a first meeting—and no to a relationship— because I know, accept, and believe I am worthy of enjoying sex as pleasure only. I thought Daniel was worthy of sharing my most intimate vulnerabilities.

Today, this is how I care for my sexual, physical, mental, spiritual, and emotional health. I will always choose to be unapologetically myself, and that is true self-acceptance.

Self-worth is knowing your value. To know your own worth is to value yourself. When you practice self-love, you embrace your strengths and weaknesses; accept that not everyone will see you as the sexy being you are; decide to flourish despite others' judgement; and thrive by showing appreciation to yourself. Only then can you help others embrace their worth. After that, you must follow through and live your worth in action.

Self-Healing

How can you tell the difference behind your egoic voice and your pure, sexy, divine voice? The truth is, you cannot always know, but the more you acknowledge, accept, and live in awareness of your dark side, the more you can trust your instincts. You have to make your best effort to know the difference between the two. Be willing to be tested.

As you get to know yourself and begin to trust yourself, you will realize that your inner voice is always talking to you and guiding you. By being mindful in the moment, you're more able to hear Spirits talk to you.

I am blessed to have many animals in my home. All my pets are healers. My very fat lazy house cat Auggie, who is the newest member of the family, is also very in tune with human emotions. On a recent visit from India, my parents started calling Auggie "Billu," which means "cat" in the Punjabi language. My folks have gone back home, but Auggie still responds to "Billu" and knows when he has to help me heal.

Whenever I am sad, one of my fur babies will come and find me and cuddle with me. This immediately helps me feel better. True healing happens when you forgive yourself for your own errors in judgement. You can heal yourself and give yourself the love you are worthy of receiving, and so often try to give others.

You may go through hardships in life and may sometimes end up suffering a disconnect with yourself and your self-image. Suffering exists in life, but it's not the only thing. Pain is an important part of growth: accept and acknowledge it. Each situation you face in life, whether painful or filled with joy, can help you grow and increase your personal power. Pain is universal, we all have it, but suffering is a choice we make. Even when you are facing challenges, you must remember to celebrate your self-worth every day.

Evolution through Acceptance

Have you ever read about how a butterfly transforms itself? It starts as the humble caterpillar, that spins itself into a cocoon, then finally, after a period of time, it emerges as a beautiful butterfly. For me, the process is the same. When I am overcoming deep wounds—mostly losses—I like to go into hiding. I had a recent personal loss in the family, a death from cancer, of a mother-like figure, that pulled me into another bout of depression. I had to be very mindful during this time and tell myself that my emotions were not permanent. Grief is a process; the grief never fully goes away; it just changes over time. Consider the fact that one does not always "get over" someone's death but rather learns to deal and handle those emotions better with time. Death and birth are two similar aspects of life, and we have no real control over either of them.

Being mindful about my sad emotions, my grief and the subsequent change that it brought to my life made me realize that change helped me to be better than yesterday. Instead of self-pity, I reminded myself there is no champagne at a pity party.

You can focus your energy and time on accepting what is reality and becoming better than yesterday. Move forward with the belief that tomorrow will be better than today. Freedom comes from expanding your perspective and accepting your new reality.

Struggling with Patience

As I have mentioned before, I accept that I am not the most patient person. I want everything done, yesterday! Writing this book has been quite an experience. It has tested my patience.

Initially, I wanted this book published in December of 2017. Of course, when the time came to review the book, it was not ready to be published. Then, I gave myself a new date: January 2019. Again, the book was not ready to be published. I attribute this to the fact that patience is considered to be a passive trait, otherwise known as yin energy.

My goal is to maintain balanced yin and yang energy, and find my equanimity. For someone like me, who is a doer, moving dates around has taught me a lot about patience. I wanted the book to be perfect, so I had to wait. Lesson learned. My circumstances taught me to acquire some of the skills needed, and to be patient with myself. Balance in everything!

You can accept that you are doing the best you can. Every day in your life is a celebration of yourself, your beauty, your flaws, and your awesomeness. Each morning is a new start, and what you do today, now, in this very moment, is how you create your future. You can use reminders and affirmations of your patience in your daily life. For example, whenever I look at my bracelet—I generally wear red bracelets on my wrists because red is my lucky colour and serves as a reminder of my power energy within me—I practice being mindful of the two words imprinted on it: *Sexy Brilliant*. You too can practice mindfulness relentlessly.

Acquiring patience is a skill that is new to me. Perhaps you too have something similar to improve? Accepting all of yourself—as in, no part of yourself is the enemy—is the key to a sexier version of yourself. The more you know and accept yourself, the more of yourself you can love.

Self-love is the ability to love yourself no matter what: patient or impatient, fat or skinny, loud or quiet. Impossible, some may say. Why? What stops you from loving yourself?

The biggest hurdle is often the feeling that you're too flawed, and therefore unlovable. In fact, you are perfect just the way you are, as the Divine meant for you to be. If you don't appreciate your own divine being, how will others appreciate you? Research tells us that people who practice self-love are happier and have higher self-esteem. By accepting yourself in your current state of perfection, you can get out of your own way in order to live a blissful life.

Only you control your own attitudes, feelings, choices, and destiny. You always have the power to change yourself. Self-love is the prerequisite to happiness. Is self-love the same as selfishness? No! In fact, loving yourself allows you to love others and to give of yourself. In this way, self-love leads you to be more generous with your partners, families, communities, and the world. Living in awareness that I lack patience is knowing myself. Then comes accepting myself; only then, can I begin loving myself.

The journey to more self-love is love itself.

My Full-Time Hobby

Not every marriage has a happy ending. Not all love stories are magical. Not all couples end up with a fairy tale ending, together for eternity. Not all lovers end up being soulmates, but love is still the essence of life. Emmanuelle Riva quotes: "Love is the essence of life; love touches all of our work. Love never leaves us. It clings to us, and we cling to it."

Having made dating my hobby and passion for the past seven years, I have become really clear on my relationship and dating goals. I learned to be honest about those goals with myself and others. If I'm looking for sex, I say so. If I'm not interested in a long-term commitment, I'm clear about my position. If I'm looking for a partner who enjoys dog-walking and outdoor activities, I don't go out with an indoor-loving, animal-hating date. Whenever the opportunity to find a human connection appears, I will be honest with both of us.

About five years ago, I met and shared a brief relationship with a teacher named Scott. He was a tall, single father with blue eyes. Scott and I had a sweet time, even though I was going through a transition at that time in my life. Our connection was beautiful, but our ambitions were so different. He was happy to have a job as a schoolteacher. He didn't own a passport. He didn't have a desire to learn about or see the world. His goal was to retire at the age of 55 on a secure pension. Our life visions were completely different.

I still hadn't found my life purpose of Sexy Brilliance, but I knew that I was too ambitious to be with Scott in the long-term. Our relationship had everything except symmetry of our life wishes and plans. Those were different.

Walking away from Scott was something I didn't enjoy doing. I asked myself why I couldn't be happy with Scott. I really beat myself up. I blamed myself. *Why do I have to be so ambitious? Why can't I tone it down?* And so on. I didn't like myself when it meant walking away. However, regardless of the fact that he was an honest, decent, man and the connection was great, I knew that our interests and ambitions did not fit. No amount of trying was likely to end in a symbiotic partnership.

Looking back, Scott was another lesson in my life that taught me the need to accept my ambitious side, in order to make the best decisions for myself.

If you want people to be honest with you, you must know yourself. You need to identify your likes and dislikes to accept them and vice-versa. This will help in giving you clearer intentions for yourself and others.

Self-Love

Scott was very kind to me. We ended our relationship in an amicable way. I was firm yet kind in my decision. Honesty should never be a choice: it should always be mandatory.

It's easy to let unkind people take you out of your element.

The truth is, everyone is going through their own suffering. The way others act is not a reflection of your value. Sure, it stings when you run into an unkind individual. It's helpful to acknowledge those feelings, forgive, and continue in a manner true to your life path. You should definitely send out awesome, kind vibes. They usually come back, multiplied.

Life is too short to let anyone else keep you from living your best life as the empowered and enlightened being that you are.

To love others fully and act with kindness, you need to master self-love. For much of my life, I didn't know anything about self-love. I looked for love outside of myself. I looked everywhere. I searched for love from online dating sites to matchmaking events to vegan restaurants to religious institutes to personal ads.

I also notice that the same is true in the people I talk to, collaborate with, and interview. People are all social animals, and often need relationships with the outside world to feel validated.

You do not need to rely solely on outside validation, but you must pay attention to how others treat you. Every interaction is either supporting or limiting. The best evidence of what people truly feel and believe comes less from their words and more from their actions.

You can strive to surround yourself with authentic people and experiences. You can always ask yourself, How does this person make me feel? How does that event make me feel? If someone or something is not making you feel good about yourself and your choices, find something else that will. In each moment, you're empowered to do things differently in order to feel better and more connected to your soul.

Every time you listen to your inner voice, you will do the right thing and make the right change.

Love Is My Mother Tongue

You may have already guessed that dating has always been my

favourite pastime. Perhaps it's my only hobby. I am a super social person, and one of the things that I have always enjoyed is spending time with new and different people. There is always something to learn about myself and the world that I live in. Personally, I am never impressed by university degrees, job titles, social media followings, or fancy cars. Instead, I am impressed by how humble a person is and how they treat others.

A text conversation between me and Geoff, a reserved university professor—someone with both a master's degree and a doctorate in science—illustrates how this affects my interactions with others. He used fancy English words when he spoke that I was not familiar with.

One conversation in particular unfolded like this:

Me: "I'm sorry but I have never heard this word before, let me search this. English isn't my first language."

Geoff: "I am sorry! I didn't mean to intimidate you."

Me: "I am not intimidated, but I did fail high school." [I said this intentionally, hoping to discourage further contact. What could we possibly have in common?]

Geoff: "What is your mother tongue?"

Me: "LOVE."

Geoff: "Wow. I like you. How soon can you meet me?"

I was surprised Geoff really wanted to meet me. I actually was a little bit intimidated by his professional designations. Then, I had to talk myself through my doubts and remind myself that I really am who I attract. Geoff must see me as worthwhile of his time; otherwise, why did he want to make an effort to get to know me?

Now, Claudia did try to sabotage this first date from the very start. I just knew that my parents would start pressuring me to marry Geoff immediately if they were to ever meet him. He was exactly what they looked for in a son-in-law. On some level, I also expected Geoff to run far, far away. His interest in me was an eye opener for me. From that brief exchange with Geoff, it gave me the confidence to go forward, and I decided to be fully, authentically, ridiculously *me*.

There are so many things that I learned from Geoff. I was still evolving into the woman that I am now. In the beginning, I allowed my assumptions and insecurities to impact my relationship dynamic. Then, when my fears and insecurities failed to sabotage our encounter, I was able to find the courage to open up and speak from my heart. I finally allowed my intuition to take the lead. I walked away from the experience having learned many lessons.

I know it reads like a cliché when I say that love is my mother tongue. Even as I think about it, it makes me laugh. I can see how ridiculous it might sound. But I truly believe that love is all that matters. The rational, scientific method is great at breaking things down into small pieces and examining the effects of a single factor. However, when it comes to love, even a scientific mind like Geoff's can be open to the possibilities. This potential mate liked how the "love" emotion made him feel, and that's something that is challenging to quantify with science. Although we shared more differences than similarities, we were both open to the possibility of love.

When I texted Geoff that love was my mother tongue, I had no hidden agenda or plan. Instead, my expression was just as perfect as it happened, which is the way I choose to view every moment of my life, in the *now-ness*. The moment was borne of inspiration and intuition from my inner voice. However, after I spoke the words, I realized that they truly reflected my beliefs and values.

"Mother tongue" is a phrase I enjoy using, and after that experience, I continued to identify love as my native language. My life was not always all about love. It has been a journey to get here. But now, I choose love as my only language.

Love truly is our mother tongue.

Loving without Words

What are some ways that you can express love to others without using words? I once took a university class in human relations where our assignment involved non-verbal communication. I remember having to sit still for five minutes with a classmate. Our assignment was to write about the challenges of non-verbal communication. I had to look into my partner's eyes and focus on the color of their irises.

It has been nearly 15 years, yet I remember how uncomfortable I felt doing this assignment. I was not alone: the whole class was fidgeting, and we all felt out of our comfort zone. I learned and now recognize and accept that eye contact is very impactful. It's a moment of true vulnerability to open yourself, become receptive and intimate, and allow others into your space. You accept that the person you are gazing at is the only person in the world at that moment.

This is a great exercise to try: keep your mouth closed and only listen. Watch for the other person's breathing. The ability to listen is a gift.

How do you listen when you're alone? How can you use this same principle to love yourself?

You can direct your receptive energy to your inner voice that is always guiding you toward sexiness. The more you listen to your inner voice, the stronger it becomes, and the more you can shine in your brilliance. Some skills can be acquired over your lifetime. Learning is lifelong. You can develop, evolve, and acquire new talents for as long as you are here on this planet!

Keep Self-Talk Positive

Using the Mirror Therapy tool from the last chapter's activity, you learned the power of positive self-talk. Turning that around, you should now know that, just as you should not hurt others with your words, you should not put yourself down, either.

In accepting yourself, you can accept others. You're in charge of your life. Therefore, it's up to you to love and appreciate your own body and mind.

As you become more empowered in your journey of becoming Sexy Brilliant, you may hear statements like, "You're not the center of the world." But, in fact, each of us is the center of our own universe: all that you call life unfolds as a result of how you think, feel, intend, speak, and act on the world. You owe it to yourself, and to the universe, to think abundantly.

Universal Abundance

When you can accept yourself, you will experience change in your life, your relationships, and how you handle money. I had a bit of a cash flow crunch while I was studying real estate, and it was a very sobering experience to seek short-term financing.

Through my own humbling experiences, I have learned that I should not focus my energy on lack of money. If you decide to return to college or school or learn something new or change your vocation, the universe will provide it for you. Rather than worry about money, focus on *being*, and what will come from your efforts. Money is just another form of energy.

We all need money to navigate our way through the modern world. Have you ever wondered why, for some, money seems to come so easily while for others it's a constant source of struggle and stress? Whether you desire a new career or additional skills that feel right to you, you must follow your calling. For some, money matters more to them than it does to others. One thing is for sure: if you don't take care of your money matters, it will matter more to you than you want it too.

How healthy is your relationship with money? Do you

make space in your life for money? Are you married to money or just casually dating it? Life is a gift. You are constantly given many opportunities to learn and to empower yourself. You must embrace change and say yes to life's new adventures. Energy follows intention, and for you to experience positive energy, it's imperative to think abundantly.

Welcoming Anxiety and Fear

I accept that I have fears. Like all human beings, I'm afraid of failure. I'm also afraid of losing or being hurt. You can accept your distress and still be willing to take a risk and open your heart, soul, and body to new experiences, hopes, and dreams.

Every time I have an anxiety attack, I tell myself that I'm going to activate my courage. I move forward and take the next step. That, to me, is so very powerful. Every experience is a chance to start all over again and to learn something new. Setting aside trepidation is key to being sexy.

As I make positive choices to balance my home and work life with abundance, I offer one piece of guidance for others: be present *now*. It will make you a better parent as well as a better worker. Children live an authentic and free life. They would much rather have a parent who is fully present while they are with them, even if it is for a brief time frame, rather than have overstressed parents who are physically present but never available.

Now is the only moment that matters. There is love in *now-ness*. There is abundance in this mindset: when you acquire it, it will trickle into every aspect of your life.

This is what I have learned and accepted. I view life in its *full*ness, in the present moment.

Goofy Girls

Part of being sexy is learning how to be playful. Once you

go goofy, you never go back!

Think about it: once you have sex with someone who has the ability to make you laugh, you just do not go back to living without that. Physical intimacy without laughter is just plain old boring. Funny people are sexually more attractive. The best sex I have had is with someone who can make me laugh. My personal goal is to laugh one hundred times a day and I do spend a lot of my time laughing, and that is what makes me Sexy Brilliant.

If the sex is good and if you can laugh after, that is another orgasm right there! Playful means the ability to laugh at yourself. When you are being playful, you can work your magic with happiness and laughter.

It's Okay to Be Eccentric

An important part of being Sexy Brilliant is accepting your imperfections, brilliance, and shine. These qualities are also called eccentricities.

I am the most eccentric person I know. Lately, if someone asks me what I do, I describe myself as an eccentric butterfly. The butterfly is a symbol of me, coming into myself. It signifies that I am free: free to be honest to myself.

Authenticity is a journey that starts with self-awareness of everything that I have done and created for myself. I accept that I created my own life instinctively. My inner voice is very strong; being able to connect with my inner child has helped me embrace my dark and light sides.

Eccentricity makes my life very interesting.

Are not all brilliant people at least a little mad? I am definitely someone who has a little bit of madness to them. I am mad! I am kooky! I am wacky! I love that about myself.

The easiest thing in life is to live within your comfort zone. The unknown is always the most challenging. I am stepping out of my comfort zone in writing my first book. And that is madness: a drive to do something unconventional, but I know that my purpose is bigger than myself.

I accept that my brilliance is in being sexy. Instead of holding down a comfortable job, I always choose to do something risky. Never be afraid to take up new challenges; that's how we learn our own true power and gain inner confidence. Have you accepted your brilliance? Do you know what makes you feel sexy?

Self-Respect Is Sexy

As my small business, which started with dog-walking grew, I turned down opportunities that were not profitable enough, choosing instead to retain my high-paying clients. I kept building and building.

With clients in pet care, senior care, and property management, my business expanded beyond my available capacity. I made the choice that I would rather work with kind, polite clients, rather than taking on extra clients who were difficult. I retained clients who were respectful even though I was their dog walker—a good reminder that respect should never be an option.

Even in business, authenticity is mandatory. As my business grew, I realized that I could not be everywhere at the same time. I started delegating work to staff members. Finding and training people who were more capable and efficient than me was a way of recognizing and accepting my own shortcomings. It was key to entrepreneurial growth.

You are gifted in your own unique way. Yes, you surely can do everything you set your mind to, but nobody is good at doing everything, all at the same time. The goal of every entrepreneur should be to hire, work, and learn from someone smarter, talented, and more capable than them. This is action based in acceptance. When someone from my team does well, I am genuinely pleased for them. Their success is my success, and vice-versa.

I strive to provide a safe, comfortable, and tolerant work environment, full of respect. One time, Jenny, my most reliable assistant, was taking care of a property for me. It was late on a Sunday afternoon while I was away in the countryside. Jenny called me in panic, telling me that she lost the keys and was unable to lock up the office.

My first instinct was to panic along with her. Instead, I asked about her safety. Once she assured me she was safe, I told her, "We can always replace a lock and keys. We cannot replace you, Jenny."

My acceptance and support reassured Jenny that she would not lose her job because of this incident. Later on, Jenny was able to locate the keys with the help of her friends. The matter was resolved rather quickly.

When I look for other people to collaborate with, I look at how they treat people around them: how they talk about their co-workers and their ex-partners. I use the same process for all my potential business and professional meetings.

Do not tolerate disrespect, especially from yourself.

Accepting Your Calling

I passed on some very lucrative business opportunities and even film roles to write this book. As I wrote, I knew writing was my life purpose. It was the right choice.

You are meant for greatness: you will find it in your calling. Part of my journey is meant to help myself by unveiling my stories in a spirit from which you can also benefit. You must help yourself before you can help others. My calling was to write this book.

How do you know your calling? How can you identify the one thing you are meant to do, above all else? Your calling is your instinct telling you to do something. In my case, my instinct and my inner voice are both very strong.

Every time I have not listened to my inner voice, I have regretted it. The inner voice is not logical. My rational brain always tells me to go back to what is expected of me. It directs me back to my office and the 9-5 hustle. However, this is not what my heart desires.

The rational mind is not strictly a negative thing. Somehow, you must create coherence between the rational mind and the desires of your heart. Get them working together on your behalf. As you already know, I have a name for my rational mind: Claudia. Claudia is ambitious. Claudia is both fear and fearlessness. She represents my extremes. Claudia is a paradox. The rational mind is a part of me, and I have to know how to dance with my ego. I acknowledge Claudia's existence, but do not let her control me.

Your thoughts are probably always telling you that you must worry about finances and accumulate wealth. That is how ego often brings worry and stress into life. From the perspective of logic alone, I'm making a mistake by writing this book. However, my intuition is happy to ignore logic. Instead, it is making me type these words.

As I type, all I see are possibilities. I see my book read by billions and billions of people: four billion people, approximately half of the global population. I see this happening five years from the date of its publication. Why did I say four billion, and not everyone? Simply, I am ambitious, but not greedy.

My visualization process works best when I have numbers, dates, and public proclamations in my strategy. I visualize my upcoming television show.

Remember what I said about self-knowledge and ego? Claudia is constantly creating drama in my life. She is the reason I am so good on-screen, and she is also why I have the self-knowledge that I do. I work with her when I visualize the success of my television show. Then, my work comes from a deep understanding of my talents and ability and the importance of my message.

Again, my ego is not a bad thing. Rather, it's a part of my identity. Naming my ego was a positive way to practice self-acceptance.

Loving your ego helps you be less afraid of your darkness.

Love Your Ego

After years and years of struggle, I know that Sexy Brilliant™ Global Revolution is my divine calling. I choose to listen to my inner voice. I heed my intuition. I keep writing, even though my stomach is in knots as I type these words and my hands are shaking.

There are so many intimate details to share, and I feel shy and embarrassed to expose myself this way. However, I know the sexy divine is asking me to follow through. Even though I feel petrified each time I share my vulnerabilities, more importantly, I know that courage is always one step ahead of fear! Knowing and accepting myself creates wisdom that I have continued to carry with me.

Even when I am making business decisions, instead of writing, my intuition is leading the way and providing more clarity in my life. Intuition puts me into contact with people who will remind me to have courage and believe in my dreams. Fear is my ego telling me that I am making a mistake by quitting my former career, but I take courage knowing that the only voice I need to listen to is my inner voice.

Life Is a Party

The other day I was talking to one of my good friends, Neeta.
She said to me, "Life is so difficult."

I looked at her and answered, "Life is a party."

She was surprised. "I cannot see it as a party, because I only see difficulty," she said.

I accept that difficulty is not fun, and it doesn't always make you feel like rejoicing as you would at a party. I was deeply depressed during this period of my life, and Neeta's perspective was tempting, even though I knew it was not true. I asked Neeta to replace the word "difficulty" with the word "challenge."

The words you use are powerful. I look at life as a party: sometimes a good party, and sometimes not such a good party. When I go through depressive mood swings, it is not such a good party. When I go through tough times, I take care of my emotional, physical, mental, sexual, and spiritual health to the best of my ability. How? By celebrating, being aware, and accepting every situation in a holistic manner as it is. I try to find joy, even if I'm depressed.

As I get to know myself better, I realize that the qualities I cherish in myself are also what I seek in a partner: true honesty, keen friendship, and shared family values. I also value a state of personal awareness and high emotional and spiritual intelligence.

You too, can learn to see life as a party, no matter how low you feel. When you do this, you will find yourself less afraid to unveil your authentic self.

Activity: Chapter Six

Everyone thinks that darkness is a negative thing. The ego's power is considered dark. Society erects a taboo around the ego, labeling it as a negative force. I, on the other hand, being a rebel, have lovingly befriended my ego, Claudia.

Claudia is fearless and daring. She drives my ambition. Because of her, I have doses of drama that add spice to my life. The trick is not letting your ego control you. The more you love your darkness, the more you will learn to dance with it. You might even start to enjoy the rhythm!

Just as in an orchestra, your ego's music sounds best when all its parts are in sync. It is time to be part of the orchestra— dare to be the conductor!

So, who is your Claudia? Name him, her, or them! Remember, you will be spending a lot of time with your ego, so you might as well give them a name you like.

My ego's name is:

_____

What does your ego do that is extreme, compared to who you are, day-to-day?

_____

_____

_____

How can your ego's excesses benefit you? How would your life change if you befriended and started having a loving relationship with them?

_____

_____

_____

_____

Open the doors to your darkness. You know you can always shed some light on it! But remember, too much brilliance can make you blind! I am so blessed that when I get blinded by my own brilliant light, I get lessons to keep me in check. These lessons keep coming back in different shapes and sizes until I learn from them.

What is your weakness or blind spot?

_____

_____

_____

_____

Now, let's talk about baggage. Imagine that you can see it, and visualize your baggage as rocks that weigh you down. It holds you back and darkens your brilliance. Each rock varies in weight, depending on what and how much importance it has in your life.
Write down the names and origins of all the rocks that you carry, everywhere you go.
How many kilograms? How many pounds are you holding

on to and how has it affected your self-esteem? Your body image? Your mental state, friendships, love life, potential partnerships, and professional life? Who are you angry at? Write down everything that comes to mind. Although it can be painful, it's important to identify what is holding you back.

Rock 1	Category	Your weight _____ kg/lbs
Rock 2	Category	Your weight _____ kg/lbs
Rock 3	Category	Your weight _____ kg/lbs
Rock 4	Category	Your weight _____ kg/lbs
Rock 5	Category	Your weight _____ kg/lbs
	Total Weight =	

Now that you have identified your baggage, it's time to forgive and forget. Forgiving forward. For giving forward. Get it?

It all starts with asking for self-forgiveness. An ancient Hawaiian practice of reconciliation and forgiveness called Ho'oponopono has been known to create powerful outcomes. Adapting its mantras can help you let go of your emotional baggage, cultural stigmas, and ancestral ties. Forgiveness is difficult, but it does not have to be so. Discover the taste of freedom when you silently repeat these simple, but powerful phrases:

- I love you
- I am sorry
- Please forgive me
- Thank you

Repeat these words as you work through each item on your list. Feel yourself become lighter as you leave your past behind and claim your Sexy Brilliance, for now and for the future.

Chapter Seven: Unveil

In the previous chapter, you learned to accept and love yourself as you are, in this very moment's state of perfection. Nothing that is repressed really goes away. It just sits there and festers and consequently multiplies. But what happens after you know and accept yourself? Now it's time to unveil. Unveiling the parts of yourself that you uncover when you know and accept yourself is the third step in the K.A.U.R.™ process.

You do not have to share everything with everyone, but you will discover some things in yourself as you go deeper. Unveiling will help you connect with the parts of yourself that are sometimes hard to face and to examine. You may find insecurity, jealousy, unhealthy relationship patterns, or addiction, to name a few things that sometimes lurk under the surface. Unveiling yourself means you do not live in discontent anymore. Taking this step means you have chosen to embrace those parts of yourself, and have unapologetically committed to love them into health.

Addiction was a major piece of my life that I had to bring into the light. Through my experiences with knowing and accepting it, I could go through the process of unveiling.

Unveiling with Love. Take a deep breath. Let it out. Release everything that is preventing the sexy star in you from shining. Unveiling is the same thing: allowing life to flow freely through your body. Eventually, you will be able to release into the world all the energy that life has given to you to become your best self. For me, I share anything that scares me and makes me feel ashamed, even on social media. Why would I purposely make myself uncomfortable in this way? Because I know that when I deny parts of myself, I cut myself off from the flow of my own well-being.

As you have seen in the previous chapters, not knowing yourself entirely is a form of self-harm. In wearing society's mask and adopting its labels, and by not accepting your greatness, you do more damage to yourself than if you had just faced the part of yourself you wanted to run away from. In essence, in the process of unveiling, you are being your truest self in its fullest expression. You miss out on life when you deny, ignore or hide who you really are. What makes you unique? What makes you shine? What makes you stand out? Unveiling is the creation and practice of your new identity. Your actual, real identity. By showing your true colours, you authentically live the gift of your life. You do not just exist anymore; you live.

Doing inner work and holding yourself to your own authentic standards allow you to live your best life. Your personal development growth benefits both you and those around you. It provides a multi-layered opportunity to create a wonderful life as you work on shedding the old and stepping into the new.

The deep work you practice as part of the K.A.U.R.™ process requires that you are unapologetic and honest with yourself and others. This means being vulnerable, which can be a highly uncomfortable place to be in. Yet, through vulnerability comes an opportunity for power and freedom. You can cultivate vulnerability by being authentic all the time. You must be daring. Of course, in the human form, you may face apprehension. I am no different. Any time worry presents itself, I ask, "Where is this fear-based behaviour in me coming from?" Then, I tap into my innocence: the same innocence that allows a child to be a child. To do this as an adult helps me stay vulnerable.

Relationship Career

While other people have careers and work-related goals, I am embarrassed to say that I have had a dating career.

Many people have addictive personalities, and may unknowingly thrive on living slightly on the edge. I am no exception. Earlier in my dating career—and it has been a career—the problem seemed to lie with me looking for someone outside of myself to save me. In fact, I was addicted to unhealthy relationships. I have evolved since then. I now acknowledge this addictive aspect of my personality and practice radical self-care as a means to fulfill myself, instead of looking to be fulfilled by others. It's so rare for me to find genuine connections with other people. I search for them avidly; as a human being, I naturally want to connect. I have an innate desire to share my authentic self with others, to unveil. The unveiling process works in my favour when I proceed with courage and self-love.

Recently, I was introduced to Jacques by some of my friends. Over a few days, he and I chatted and made plans to take it further. Then, all of a sudden Jacques messaged me. He had seen me on television talking about my addictive dating and said that he was not interested in meeting me anymore, as he didn't appreciate my behaviour. Rather, he thought I had wasted his time.

I thanked him for unveiling his true feelings to me, rather than wasting my time. This type of rejection becomes the food for my success, based on my acceptance of it. I grew because I accepted that Jacques was not willing to accept myself as me. I did not need to apologize for my behaviour or my honesty. I was true to myself and forgiving of myself through practicing radical self-acceptance when I shared who I was, and my honesty protected me from attempting to connect with someone who was not meant to be a part of my Sexy Brilliant life. Our present-day need to be accepted by our culture and our society has conditioned us to become consumers based on our emotions. Jacques was no different; based on his internet research of my television experience, he had already formed a judgement of me. I share my experiences because they will perhaps connect me to many of you. I seek authentic connection in a commercialized world.

Our emotions are the perfect target for commercialization. Think about the advertising you are exposed to daily. Happy? Have an alcoholic beverage or a sugary drink. Ill or uneasy? Pharmaceutical companies tap into your fear of sickness and death by making and advertising medicines to cure various diseases. I make a conscious effort to keep these advertisements in perspective. One of the things I choose is not to consume alcohol because I know it would be very easy for me to get addicted. This is also true for other substances, food, sex, people, pain, depression, and so on. I know myself, and I know I have an addictive personality. Even when I am at social events, I decline a glass of wine, because I don't want to use an outside source to change the way I feel. It would not be long before I was using it to deny my pain and suffering. Now, I am not suggesting that alcohol is bad or good. In fact, nothing is intrinsically good or bad, everything just is. The important thing is to recognize when something does not have a positive effect on you and wastes your time, emotions, and energy. For me, I am deeply sensitive. I am affected by the global tragedies that I hear about on the news, so I am very careful about the news that I choose to consume. The more tragic the news I listen to, the more depressed I feel. This is just one example. Perhaps you have certain events or people that add negative energy to your life as well. I do not want to spend my life stuck in counterproductive behaviour, so I act accordingly. When you love yourself, you feel worthy of good care, which includes protecting your energies from lower vibrational influences of all kinds.

Achievement Addiction

It is critical to learn how to differentiate between what is important for your health and what is a distraction and even escapism. As I was finishing the editing process of my book, I got the news that I was accepted into a creative writing program in Europe. (Did I mention that I am a full-time student of life?) Part of my H-Factor, as I mentioned, means that I am always hungry for more learning. Often, addictions are a result of our ego taking control. When you are truly empowered, you know, accept, and believe in your worth. You unveil your true self by acknowledging distractions, thus allowing yourself to shine like a sexy being in making good decisions.

Your past is a part of your future. Your past experiences have made you who and what you are today. Using the word "addiction" to describe my extreme pursuit of education makes sense to me. That addiction was linked to my addiction of collecting achievements and praise. Although there have also been positive results from choosing to pursue higher education, there's no question that it's a double-edged sword. A while back, I made the decision to go back to college for a degree in communications. I signed up for one year of full-time studying, while managing a home, a family, and a business. It is something that I wanted to do for myself to gain more knowledge, and of course, yet another diploma. The course started with nineteen students. Halfway through the program, five students dropped out. The program was not for everyone. By the end, only nine students were left. The course was so demanding that maintaining a life-work balance became nearly impossible. As the end of the semester approached, a few people realized that studying was too difficult. Some even decided that this was not helping them learn something new. They dropped out. The rest of us continued the program despite family, health, and work-related commitments. In the end, each of us had to make a decision about what was best for our own situations. Perseverance helped me to complete the program. My classmates' choice to quit could be seen as a failure to complete something; however, the truth is that they were simply making a decision. They unveiled their values and proceeded on a different path that worked better for them.

Again, there are no right or wrong decisions, but decisions must be made in order to move forward successfully. Embrace this Sexy Brilliant™ moment of freedom: no matter what you are doing, you can change your mind. Even after a decision has been made, you can always change directions as you acquire and accumulate additional knowledge about a situation. You are absolutely entitled to make new decisions and reverse old ones, based on the fresh perspectives and information you receive. Unveiling yourself to others can be intimidating. You may fear judgement, but facing the fear and stepping into the light will help you shine.

Food Addiction

I have had a lifelong struggle with food. My food addictions come from the constant food anxiety I grew up with in my family. The issue was not scarcity. Rather, my food and eating habits were monitored constantly. I was consistently reminded that I was too fat and that nobody would marry me if I did not lose weight.

It's never alright for families to tell their children, or for you to tell yourself, that nobody will love you because of your size, or your personality, or for any reason. As a mother, I cannot imagine conveying the same messages to my child.

Marriage and relationships are personal, heart-centered decisions revolving around love. Physical size does not affect anyone's lovability. Also, your happiness does not depend on your marital status. I needed to work hard to change this mindset; I want my daughter to be empowered, as I was not. As you can imagine, I felt unlovable and unworthy of healthy relationships. This is where the food struggle began. I am an emotional eater and I do eat my feelings. The difference now is my awareness of what I am actually doing and eating. I accept my emotions, which keeps them from controlling me.

An eating disorder and food addiction can affect anyone regardless of age, background, race, gender, or socioeconomic status. It's important to be self-sufficient, but it's also perfectly acceptable to ask for help. Remember that when you struggle with food addictions, you are not alone. It's never too late to get help. You are worthy of love, even when you feel like you are not.

It took me a long time to realize that I have a food addiction. The first step was to acknowledge that I had a problem. One night, when I was about twenty-three years old, I dove into a big pile of feelings: three litres of chocolate ice cream. I had been rejected at a job interview and then immediately went through yet another failed relationship. There I was, binge-eating ice cream. I was so distraught that I forgot to put the almost-full container of ice cream back in the fridge. When I woke up the next morning, the ice cream had all melted. The living room was a disaster. A sticky puddle of sugar and dairy. I remember how it looked, and I always will. I remember the mess. I remember the guilt. I remember the shame. I remember wanting to kill myself because of what I was doing to my body and myself. From that day on, I made a conscious effort to separate my emotions from food. I became more aware. Once I became attentive to my food habits, I promised myself that I would never again abuse my body and myself with food in this way. Not to mention that cleaning up my mess in the living room took weeks and weeks. I remember cleaning and sobbing, sobbing and cleaning. It was a release: I had to recognize that I had a food addiction. I still cry when I think about this image, and it's still scary to unveil these darker, less desirable pieces of myself.

Moving forward in my new awareness, I learned about food labels and the products I put into my body. I eat organic, ayurvedic—a form of alternative medicine with historical roots in the Indian subcontinent—and raw food whenever possible. I avoid gluten. Granted, I eat a little differently on the road than I normally do at home. It's important to point out that sometimes I slip up, and that's fine. I acknowledge this, and I am more open to expressing myself through food. When I have a setback, I gently remind myself that it's okay and that I can restart tomorrow. I give thanks for what I did and how I behaved today. I give thanks for this awareness. I give thanks for my ability to recognize emotions related to food. Practising constant self-forgiveness helps me move on to reclaiming my sexy brilliance.

Sex Addiction

My sexual energy has always been high, or so I thought. However, my addiction to validation and difficulty forming healthy relationships are actually connected to the sexual trauma I experienced as a young woman. At the age of thirteen, I was easy prey for someone in a position of authority: a man in his forties who my family trusted. This person took advantage of me and my young age and made me feel appreciated. It started off rather innocently. He was an authority figure my family trusted. The abuse and sexual touching lasted for about nine months. While there was no penetration, there was a lot of touching, fondling and petting. He listened to me and made me feel important. It was a case of subordination. I experienced sexual abuse without knowing that it was abuse. The experience was complicated and confused me. It interfered with my sexuality for years. Like many victims of sexual abuse, I carry shame and guilt which comes from the enjoyment of a sexually experienced person touching me. I carry the trauma, because there was also pleasure. In my early twenties, I remember thinking to myself that there was something wrong with me because I was never able to enjoy sexual intercourse or have an orgasm with another person. The more sex I wanted, the less I had. I thought it was because my masculine energy was very high, having always been ambitious and driven. Looking back, it was not owing to my high masculine energy, but rather because my feminine energy was disempowered as a result of sexual abuse.

Every partner, date, and romance has ended up changing me. Whenever I am feeling a low vibration level about my past, I tell myself I had to suffer and endure so many hardships; in every experience there was an important lesson and it has allowed me to unveil and share with you. In fact, I even discussed my experience on a British television broadcast.

In my younger days, I compared my partners to one another. I would look at past partners and compare them to current partners. I would look at a younger partner and compare him to an older partner. I even compared my partners to the man who sexually abused me. Being abused had a lingering effect in so many ways. In my case, I have compared my partners to a time when I was thirteen and being sexually exploited by someone in his forties. I have often wondered how much of my addiction is tied to my experience of being sexually abused. He was there to listen to me talk about my unhappy life situations and family problems. He recognized that I was an easy target because I lacked self-esteem and self-love. My abuser gave me attention when no one else did or would. The lovemaking and seduction skills of a person who is forty is very different from a person who is thirteen, or even twenty-nine. All this time, I denied the abuse and did not deal with the trauma. I normalized the situation. I even compared other lovers to my abuser. I felt shame and the stigma of being a victim of abuse, which contributed to my unhealthy way of viewing relationships. It took years of work to unveil this experience and how it impacted me.

Keeping Secrets

I have a difficult relationship with my parents. Part of the problem is that I am not able to be myself with them. I did not allow my parents the opportunity to get close to me because of my unhealed childhood traumas. In retrospect, I felt that I really was ugly and undesirable. The sexual abuse only stopped because I moved away with my family. I never confronted my abuser. I never told my parents about it, either. Writing about this now is the first time I am unveiling what happened to me as a young girl, more than 20 years ago in India. In order to survive, I did what ostriches do. I stuck my head in the sand and pretended that it had never happened. I ignored my past until 2016, when one of my child's schoolteachers was arrested and prosecuted for possession of illegal sex tapes and pedophilia. This hit home for me, and I was shaken. I spent days crying. I was starting to relive my own teenage trauma. I had been denying that I was sexually abused. The stress and trauma of never being able to share my shame was overwhelming. I have been able to unveil this part of my past because I have sought counseling.

Many victims of abuse have a survivor mentality. We settle in whatever circumstances we find ourselves in. Everyone endures traumatic things or has tragic events in their lives. Your trauma does not have to dictate your future or dampen your brilliance. Being sexy is all about how you thrive, despite the challenges you face. I chose to go with the flow of life. For years, I did not acknowledge the abuse, but that was how I was able to cope at the time. When I became able to deal with the ramifications of what had happened, I addressed it. Then, I began talking about it so that I could use my experience to help others. I am still healing. Healing is lifelong. I like to say that I flourish in spite of—or because of—whatever life throws at me. You can flourish in spite of your misfortunes, too. You have this capacity within you. In choosing to focus on your best qualities, you create more of what you most desire in yourself and in your life. When you know, accept, and unveil your truth, you are taking action. You can refuse to keep shameful, hurtful secrets for any longer.

Dating Addiction

Related to my sexual addiction and my serious insecurity, I developed what became a dating addiction. I was loud and ambitious; yet, when it came down to relationships, I was unwilling to listen to the inner wisdom that was trying to guide me. Those of you who have been single and have ever looked for love online may understand this: *the light that I was searching for outside was actually within me.* I had read that dating could be a wonderful way of getting to know myself better. So, after the end of my arranged marriage, I excitedly began putting up online dating profiles. I entered the dating world with all my passion, even though putting myself out there was intimidating. It was something that was right for that moment in my life. It was not easy to put myself out there. I was not yet the Sexy Brilliant person that I am now. Seeking affection and attention from strangers quickly became a pattern. It was a way of finding fulfillment for the ending of my marriage.

The first time I went on a date after the end of a painful relationship, I had no idea what I was doing. I was not sure about myself. I had zero dating confidence and my self-esteem was at an all-time low. However, like all of us, I did feel deserving of love and intimacy. I spent plenty of money on the pursuit of love. Having undergone the break-up and end of my marriage and a career change, I had cash-flow issues, and online dating often comes with a price tag. I remember trying a few dating websites and having fancy ads with details on them along with beautiful pictures. I was a paid member on three dating websites, although not at the same time. Even though I tried the best-known dating websites in North America, I met exactly zero matches. Over the course of three months, I tried at least seven different dating sites and apps. I was honest and sincere in my search for a connection. I remember it was nearly impossible to form even a chat relationship with another person. Once I started chatting, it never transitioned to real life. At that time, it felt like nobody wanted to meet me.

Checking out dating sites everyday felt like a waste of time, because it was not getting me the results I wanted. The emotional time and energy spent on these sites can become expensive! My frustration at not finding any connection led me to even lower self-confidence.

When I realized that the dating sites were affecting my mood, I had to force myself to look at other options. Rejection after rejection was not helping me.

So, I tried what I thought might be a more unusual method: placing a personal ad online on sites like Craigslist. Even though my friends thought I was being too risky, I felt like being daring. I followed my instincts, and I went on to meet some amazing people. I searched the personal sections of these types of online forums. Since the traditional dating sites did not work for me and I had a zero-success rate, Craigslist is how I met dates for years. This experiment is one of the experiences that shows who I am. I have been fortunate enough to meet some amazing long-term and short-term partners by dating people I met on a site that advertises everything from used cars and old couches to ukuleles.

Unveiling the Devina that was ready for dating was an important moment in my life. I will connect to it for as long as I am in the flow of life. I remember the first time I met someone in the personals section. He was looking for a garage for his vintage Mercedes, and I had placed this ad:

"Hey there! I am a thirty-something fun-loving, single mother who is looking to take my dogs out for a walk this evening. Things that I look for in a potential date are: laughter, mutual respect, and most importantly, please be single. Please email with a picture, location, and a phone number. If you send me any penis pictures, I shall block you and report you for spam. Finally, if you are soliciting me for money, please know that the only thing I can give you is a good conversation on this anonymous platform."

The man with the vintage car was not the only person I met. When I placed my ad, I connected with a few people and had coffee with two men. One of them was married; the second was in a long-term relationship. A few men emailed me on the pretext of being single; however, when I finally connected a bit further and discussed plans for a dog walk or coffee, the truth came out that they were in unhappy relationships. I am not interested in being anyone's dirty secret, mistress, or way out. In my opinion, if a person is in an unhappy marriage, they should leave it—but I digress.

Dating on Craigslist helped me to learn a quick method

of verifying men and their current situations. I got hundreds of emails a day after I put that ad up. Since Craigslist is an anonymous platform, the anonymity and the mystery also make connecting more exciting. I quickly learned that if I established an email connection with someone, but did not move to a phone connection, the other person was wasting my time. It is easy to tell when someone is not genuinely interested: the potential date who does not respond to messages, the friend who is always "too busy," or the date who just does not show up.

Being your sexy self not only means attracting someone awesome, but choosing someone who has similar priorities to yours. If you are looking for a relationship, that means that the other person should be on the same page. I also learned that if a man only wanted to hang out during the day, that it most probably meant that he had commitments in the evenings—like a wife and children. A few times, men would send very old pictures, and I had to call them out on it. I learned that truly honest, single people were willing to share their pictures and phone numbers. Before I met someone face-to-face, I always insisted on speaking on the phone. Generally, this would tell me a lot about a potential partner, date or hook-up. I asked awkward questions. I was brutally honest in all my communications. When something did not feel right, I signed off. I learned to trust my own instincts and inner voice. I knew what disrespect, loathing, and criticism sounded like, and I refused to allow myself to make excuses for anyone. I accepted myself and shared myself without excuses, lies, or game-playing.

Whenever I received unsolicited penis pictures, I blocked those messages in the spam folder. I knew this was not something that would ever turn me on. Being self-aware helped me weed out and discard messages from inappropriate men. The more I invested in loving myself, the less patience I had for overly aggressive, negative, or insecure people in my life. What felt right changed as I began to see myself as worthy and valued. A good-looking boyfriend with control issues became less and less desirable to me as my self-esteem grew.

Personal Development Is Key to Success in Dating, and in Life!

Even in the personal ads, I found many honest, single, lonely people looking for cars, sex, and love. I enjoyed connecting with people. This was during a time when text messaging was not yet in fashion. I was open and willing to try new things—plus I also learned to get out of the way of my own happiness by making an effort to put myself out there. I faced my fear of dating rejection. This way, I was the only person responsible for my destiny. I was unveiling parts of myself that I would have previously denied or hidden from the light of day.

I met a few people, but no one I wanted to get naked with. You only want to get naked with people who are worthy of getting naked with, right? Things would stay this way until I met George—but that is a story for another time!

A Perfect Love

I committed to searching for my perfect love for three years. In that time, I connected with around 150 men through online personals, by phone, via text, in chance meetings, and on dates. When I started my journey, I thought my perfect love would look like the marriage that my parents share, which is full of mutual love, respect, and friendship. In fact, it was very different. This period of intense dating and searching taught me a lot about myself. I have only shared a handful of the stories and lessons I learned here. When I look back, it is hard to believe that I had the time or energy to get to know 150 men. I started this journey looking for someone to fill a need, a desire, and a void within myself. At the time, my friends were worried about me. I avoided my family and would not talk to them for days, and I really came face-to-face with the realization that I am an addict. A dating addict.

Somewhere around date 125, it became clear that what I was looking for was not to be found in a personals ad, on a bike path, or at a meet-up group. Now, I am not an expert, and I do not recommend you indulge in your insecurities to the extent that I did. I am grateful that I was able to have the experiences I did without getting hurt or hurting others. It took courage to unveil my true self to total strangers. But I did it, over and over again. It was liberating and exciting, and I do not regret a single moment. In fact, looking back at this behaviour which I indulged in in a rather extreme way, I see that dating on Craigslist gave me the gift of self-love. Many men gave me their love and affection and shared their genuine and vulnerable selves with me, as I did with them. Did they get as much out of the experience as I did? I guess I ask them: "Was it good for you?" Over the course of three years, I did actually end up dating someone who checked all the boxes of the "perfect love" I had set out to find. But unfortunately, by the time Brandon came around, I had already changed. It was too late. I had learned so much about myself through my dating addiction and my search for acceptance and love, that I was no longer looking for the perfect love. I did not need another person to make me feel complete and whole anymore. *I was there all along. It was always me.*

Unveiling myself and my needs came full circle in dating when I was able to be myself. After months of being single, looking for a connection on dating sites, and poring over Craigslist, I finally connected with a guy named Harris. An attractive triathlete with dark brown eyes. Harris was also single and looking for a connection. After a brief email exchange, we exchanged phone numbers, and eventually decided to meet at a local bike path that was halfway between our homes.

At first sight, we both liked each other. We had a great connection and spent our time laughing and enjoying nature and navigating around pedestrians, while getting to know each other. When it was time to head home, we stopped to eat ice cream and chat. We started the ride home, both agreeing that this was perhaps the best first date ever. It was a vibrant summer day in beautiful surroundings. Halfway through our bike ride home, I had to stop. I told Harris, "I need to stop and meditate in my bare feet. I am lightheaded, and I need to connect to nature. Can you please give me a few minutes alone?"

Harris was clearly surprised, but very supportive. He told me that he did not mind catching up on his emails while I took some time to myself. This was an unplanned meditation break. I had to stop to take care of myself and my emotions. My sexiness guided me to take a break from Harris's company and take time out for myself. I sensed that something was off. Perhaps it was simply too much intensity with Harris. Our kisses had been magical, and I could not wait to get to know him more in private. It was also a combination of the bicycle ride and the physical energy it took a recovering bulimic to keep up with a triathlete. Asking for time alone was a way of listening to my body and my soul. Walking barefoot in the grass helped me ground myself and take care of my own mental, emotional, spiritual, and physical needs, as well as creating space between Harris and myself. Asking a first date for some time to calm myself showed me that I can be fearless. I was brave. I did not let my fears about Harris's opinion of my odd behaviour stop me from being true to myself. I was deeply connected to myself and my needs, even though I was on a date. I listened to the little girl inside me who needed to feel like a child again, walking and meditating in the grass. I learned that unveiling my true needs was possible, and I could feel safe and happy doing so.

Healthier Habits

All of my new, healthier habits were created through overcoming my dating addiction. On a daily basis, I used to get text messages from a dozen men. These were guys that I was chatting with, in the hopes of having a relationship with one of them. By acknowledging that I had an addiction, and becoming aware that none of these men were helping me grow as a person, I came to the realization that my actions were detrimental to my own brilliance. To deal with my unhealthy habits, I had to choose to go into recovery. I had to accept that I had a problem. I would eventually unveil this problem as a part of my journey, to help others. I admitted that I was addicted to studying, dating, men, shopping, studying, and hiding from my own true self and my own brilliance. To accept help, I had to choose to be mindful in unveiling my true self to others. I faced the concepts that limited me and I discovered a new reality that was deep within me, not outside of myself.

When you listen to your inner voice and follow your instincts, you are being your true self. Being brave enough to share your authentic self is inner empowerment. When you reveal and share your brilliance, you will discover more of yourself. Be brave with your vulnerability. The perfect love I sought did not come in the form of a diploma. It did not come from any outside validation. It did not come as a paycheck. It did not come with a man, or a new career, or a new job, or a relationship. Love is a feeling; it is a gut feeling. Love lives inside of you, screaming, wanting to be heard. It comes from living truthfully, without the mask you use to keep from unveiling what you would have once tried to hide.

Sharing on Social Media

Unveiling neutralizes anxiety. It is the driving force that pushes you to get out of your comfort zone. For example, instead of fighting suicidal thoughts, I let them exist. I accept these thoughts in order to be with them. I unveil to show my flaws and weaknesses. I do not want to project the false, "perfect" version of myself. I would rather share my uniqueness. Through the acceptance of my emotional turbulence, I connect to all other human beings. In 2018, I shared a year-old picture on social media. The truth is, I was having a challenging time personally; this took the familiar form of depression. I was having intense suicidal thoughts. It was Father's Day in North America, which was triggering my depression. I love my family, but I do not always see eye to eye with them. On this particular day, I was ashamed, embarrassed, sad, weak and generally at a lower energetic vibration.

Much of my rebelliousness pushes against family pressure. My experience with suicidal thoughts on Father's Day had a lot to do with my upbringing, family programming, and cultural baggage. I was able to recognize that self-harm and suicidal thoughts were not my own, but rather, energy that I was in the process of releasing. By unveiling my thoughts, I was able to release them. I worked at clearing my energy, thoughts, and vibrations through mindfulness, meditation, self-knowledge, self-acceptance, and self-love, with the help of many professionals. If you are struggling, please do the same. The right support group will make a difference in your healing. Though unveiling can be one of the most challenging processes to practice, it can allow you to actually touch true abundance and true peace of mind.

Now, not only do I know myself, I have accepted everything that is. I will continue this process as long as I live. You cannot be embarrassed about feeling the emotions you have, showing weakness, and addressing your mental health. Depression, negative feelings, being alone, addictions, singlehood, loneliness, and mental health issues are all part of the human experience. Being ashamed of them would mean being ashamed of life. In the spiritual world, you are a beautiful soul. When you keep this in mind, you can reveal yourself to the world without fear of judgement or rejection.

Criticism Is Never Personal

When I open my emails or look at my Twitter feed, I read the not-so-good comments, along with the nice ones. Accepting criticism, even when it is inaccurate, is a part of how I am authentic and vulnerable. There will always be naysayers. I have learned that they will get louder the more genuine I become. The critics want to keep me—and consequently themselves—in a safe place. I say, good luck with that! When I invested energy in getting to know and accept my true self, I found I cared less and less about others' opinions. This sometimes made people upset—especially negative, angry people who felt threatened by my acceptance of both my flaws and theirs. How dare anyone accept weakness? How dare I threaten their sense of self by not wanting a nicer car, a bigger home, or more expensive clothing, like they do? Criticism is never personal. It is always about the person doing the criticizing. The truth is, not everyone will be able to meet you where you are in your spiritual odyssey. It is important to remember that everyone's journey is unique and individual. As a kind, self-aware human being, you must treat others with empathy and compassion. Being sexy is about being able to stay present. Be mindful of who you are and who you strive to be, in order to shine in your brilliance.

Activity: Chapter Seven

Being consistently authentic is an act of vulnerability. Be vulnerable, even when it is hard because you think people will judge you—especially then!

Adults who allow themselves to be vulnerable tend to attract others and gain their respect. Why? Because vulnerability and softness are qualities that most people have been taught to tame by parents, teachers, and leaders. Over the years, these natural emotions are moulded into a shape that does not reflect the authentic self.

So, how does one become authentic?

For this activity, you will build from the work you did in Chapter Five, about Knowing. My favourite way to create authenticity is to tap into my inner child. Where my innocence lives, there is truth. When I am connected to my inner child, I say what I feel and do what I please!

Be mindful that your inner child can sometimes drive your ego. That type of inner child refuses to let go of their dreams. Notice if it ever starts to take over. You may find yourself obsessing over a shiny object or goal until it consumes you. If this happens, re-centre yourself and try again.

What does your inner child love to do? Think back to when you were very young. Remember a time you were so happy you wished the day would not end. What were you doing? Who was with you?

_____

_____

_____

_____

_____

What is the advantage of keeping your inner child hidden?

_____

_____

_____

_____

What possibilities lie ahead if you unveil your inner child? What are the benefits of vulnerability?

_____

_____

_____

_____

Next, you will use kinesthetic learning—that is, learning through movement—to accelerate your unveiling process. Some of us like to get there quicker than others! Ready?

Outline the letter U on a sheet of paper. Draw it any way you wish. Now, notice the calligraphy. Do you think it is by chance that the letter forms waves going up and down? How simple. One stroke; it is all there.

During your unveiling process, there will be a few—actually, many—mixed emotions! Just like the letter U, you will experience highs. You may feel totally confident, standing out as your true self. You may also go through some lows: when you feel anxious, if someone judges you, or when your ego steps in. Look at the letter U. It is curved and flowing. Write the letter and feel its fluidity.
U U U u u u

_____

_____

_____

Now try writing with your other hand. For example, I am right-handed but when I colour, sometimes I use my left hand. I find myself being more patient and more mindful. It can be both fun and frustrating at the same time. Let go of the urge to use your dominant hand and try writing your name below in your second hand.

_____

With the same insight, write down three or more sentences about how you want to unveil yourself to the world. Write down three things that you have not dared doing, because of fear or limiting beliefs. For each sentence, choose a date for when it is due to happen. Time to act. Time to follow through. Less thinking—more feeling, more doing. Write, and do not judge it. Do not limit yourself. Connect to the abundance of the Universe. Unveil the courage, strength, and love that you were born with.

1.

_____

_____

Completion date: _____

2.

_____

_____

Completion date: _____

3.

_____

_____

Completion date: _____

Chapter Eight: Release

Release is the last part of your amazing journey, guided by the K.A.U.R.™ process. This final chapter also represents a new beginning; the most important since you were first born. You are on this earth because your mother pushed hard at the time of your birth. With the help of the universal force of Divinity, you were released. Suddenly, there you were.

Release is vital for living. In Release, the fourth stage of the K.A.U.R.™ process, you will experience how letting go can feel as good as an orgasm. Release is the high that you are always looking to reach.

As I release this book, I meditate and continue to clean off all unwanted energies. I work on a moment-to-moment basis. When I do my energetic cleansing, I am using the same tools that I have shared with you as the K.A.U.R.™ process. Feeling ready to release and experience everything the universe has to offer was not my way of being earlier in my life. Now, thanks to this trademarked method, I am in a constant state of being.

Grab a pen and paper and write out the number "8" by hand, in its numeral form. As you meditate on writing out the number eight, you can go into a trance. Go into a high, almost a spiritual orgasm. Accept that it's perfectly normal to be turned on by something as simple as writing a number out. It is so smooth and so curvy. It is the sexiest number to write out. It just flows. In this way, you and the number 8 are very similar. To me, writing 8 is a release. It is the number of infinity and abundance. If you are struggling financially, you can draw the number 8, the infinity number, on all your doors and windows to bring abundance into your home.

You can practice the "abundance number" in all forms to achieve release, including during sex. Using the shape of the number 8 during cunnilingus can provide powerful orgasms. Whether alone or in company, orgasms are one of the forms of release. That's why the number 8 is my absolute favourite number in bed! Do not be shy to ask for the release. Do not be shy to get the release you deserve!

Now that you know, have accepted, and have unveiled your truth, you are now ready to release your sexiness and brilliance—based on your own choices.

Internal Harmony

In today's society and in keeping with the self-help movement, people are always looking for new ways to release stress, anxiety, and pain. Releasing can mean letting go of the past. For example, one of my daily goals is to laugh one hundred times a day. Goals are goals, and even when I struggle with depression, I keep my daily goals in mind. Even my depression is sexy, because I learn about a new part of myself. In fact, people deal with massive depression in different ways. For me, crying is an emotional release and helps in letting go of the toxins in my body. However, when I am finished with tears and I have released what needs to be released, I love to laugh!

You can watch a funny movie, read a funny book, or talk to a friend with a great sense of humour. You must strive to balance your emotions and moods without being too attached to any specific emotional state. I know myself. In knowing an abundance of tears, I also know an abundance of laughter. It truly is the best medicine. Everyone heals at their own pace. As you know and accept yourself, your healing process gets progressively faster.

Laughing Is Serious

I am serious about laughter. Growing up, I was always told that I laughed too much. My family always asked me to laugh in a quiet and demure manner. I am still trying to figure out what that means! I was always warned before social gatherings to behave and not laugh as much, because social gatherings were about being proper and following the invisible social protocol. I remember my parents telling me: "A woman should be dignified, graceful, and never get too much attention. Men should be getting more attention. Remember, nobody likes too-smart women." I always laughed when I heard this particular rant. My parents would talk about equality between the sexes at home, but give me these mixed messages. In an attempt to please them, I did not behave authentically. I behaved in a way that was expected of me. Now, I have released their expectations and I laugh as much as I want to!

It has taken a lot of self-awareness to appreciate the gift of laughter. Laughing makes me happy. I choose to live in the moment, let go of my worry, and be mindful. Laughing when others might not helps me to shake off other people's conditioning. In the present day, I choose to let go of my upbringing and conditioning and laugh my way to a happier me. Ultimately, I am the one who is one hundred percent responsible for my happiness.

The same principle of release applies to relationships. Ending a relationship that is no longer helping you feel sexy or brilliant is a form of self-empowerment. I once was in a relationship with a man named George. When we broke up, I laughed. George dumped me for a woman he met online, a virtual connection. Making light of an ending does not mean that the hurt is over, but we each heal in our own way and in our own path. Being able to laugh at the happy times helps in healing faster. Since my break-up with

George, one way I have learned to cope with those feelings of loss and heartache is to enrich my life through laughter. Laughter has been found to be beneficial for our health. Laughter naturally decreases stress and gives you a sense of well-being; it also boosts your immune system, lowers your blood pressure, contributes to heart health, and helps with pain relief. While many people would not react to the loss of a healthy relationship with laughter, it was my way of coping with a tough situation. George was sad to end our partnership as well, so laughing allowed us to maintain a positive attitude through a challenging transition.

Laughter is deep and total, from within. It's a medicine that is free, natural and prescribed for all seriousness. Sometimes, you have to be a little foolish. In fact, the highest practice of wisdom often carries foolishness in it. The greatest wise men and women of the world were also the greatest fools. My daily goal of choosing to be happy is exactly why I chose laughing one hundred times a day as a release practice.

Number Two

Releasing can also mean going to the bathroom. (For a refresher, flip back to the introduction and try taking a pee break).

A few years ago, on an overnight camping trip with my running club, I was running in the wooded forests up in northern Canada. The five of us were out in the woods in the middle of summer. All of a sudden, one of my buddies disappeared into the trees. Poof—or should I say, poop! He was gone for at least ten minutes. Later on, I asked him why he was gone for so long. He laughed and said he really had to poop. He had two choices: use nature or have an accident in his running shorts. I, of course, laughed. His story ended up being a release for me as well, because I got a great laugh out of the whole scenario. I did not feel shy or ashamed. It was funny! Why carry rocks that do not belong to you? You can lay down the weight that is not yours to carry.

High on Life

Releasing is also going on holiday. What a glorious feeling! I love the anticipation of vacation. I love preparing for my trip by choosing just the right spot, packing, and finally, reaching my destination. I love having the privilege to be able to shake off the ins and outs of daily life. On vacation, you can unplug your computer and allow yourself to connect with the world around you. You can live on your time and your own schedule, without the concern of missing a work-related email or text. Holidays allow you to realign with your heart's desires. They provide another great opportunity to check in with your inner child and your most basic wants and needs. When you are in the bliss of being connected to your inner child, it's easy to feel the addictive high of life. The highs I feel are worth any of the lows I could possibly feel.

How Others Judge Me Is None of My Business

As a serial dater, I have ended up in a few relationships. Some of them lasted for a few months, and some of them lasted for years. My emotions are welling up as I write this. I feel discomfort: the fear of being judged for writing about my intimate life. Relationships are private; however, I have learned so many lessons from my addiction to dating that there is no way I will not unveil them. By sharing my story, I know I can help others.

I know I am loud and outspoken, releasing all that does not belong to me. Dating has helped me find my life purpose. Writing about my struggles with relationships and owning up to my own addictions means I open up the door for judgement. It gives me a sense of uneasiness, as I feel exposed and vulnerable. Yet, what other people think of me is not my business. My business is being true to my authentic self and sharing what I have learned. Therefore, I detach from negative outcomes, as they are not mine to own. I choose to focus on the positive, and it is my sincerest hope that as I continue to share my authentic experiences with you, you will find the inspiration to dare to live your own authentic life.

Judgement Detox

If you have developed an unhealthy habit of judging others, you will dread being judged.

Even though I have lost weight and become a healthier version of myself, it still pinches me when someone leaves me a nasty comment on a YouTube video and criticizes my size. I attempt to send those people love in response. That is how releasing other people's baggage starts. Sexiness is all about perception: I have mine and they have theirs.

How do I emotionally deal with insults and backhanded compliments? There is not a right or a wrong way of dealing with being called fat. The truth is, most people live in constant worry of being criticized by others, even if the critics are people whose opinions do not really matter. They are strangers on the Internet or on dating sites, not cherished friends. If you are afraid of being disliked or judged, you might forget to live an authentic life. Fear gets in the way of being true to yourself and your happiness. In response to that fear, my goal is to be less judgemental. I break the cycle of fear by becoming more accepting of myself and others.

Self-acceptance and acceptance of others are key to revealing a sexier version of yourself. You must be able to release your uneasiness towards judgement to be able to allow this to happen.

How you judge others is exactly how you judge yourself.

Fear of Judging Others

My journey to fearless living has taken many turns. I once dated a man for nine months. He had a micro-penis. To be very honest, we had a great sex life. We both went through many releases due to our emotional and intellectual connection. That relationship taught me that, when it comes to sexual pleasure, penis size really does not matter. The experience also taught me to be careful of judging others: things are not always what they seem. Had I discussed my boyfriend's penis size with my friends, they would have passed judgement on him and shared their comments with me. I would have had to work through not only my own issues regarding size, but also their remarks and suggestions. In reality, this man was a wonderful partner and mate. His micro-penis was not what ultimately ended our relationship. Our life stages at the time were different. He wished for the permanence of a cohabiting couple. For me, it did not feel right: my instincts guided me to say no to moving in together.

By saying no to his offer, I said yes to myself. There are no right or wrong choices, even in saying no to a relationship. Once again, I said yes to finding my life purpose. This was a powerful realization in my life. I loved myself more than ever before, because with every passing day, I was growing from within and becoming whole.

Relationships are about spiritual, emotional, and physical teamwork. Although our life stages did not match, being with this man gave me confidence. He taught me to be unapologetic about my size, my weight, and my body. I overcame my long-standing belief about size—mine and his. He met all my sexual needs, even though I almost let my prejudice get in the way of a very satisfying and growing experience.

Like many people, I had been brainwashed into believing that a bigger penis is better. What I learned from this experience is that size—just like a woman's body size or the way she dresses—does not make one a good lover or a prettier or a better person. In the end, what matters is emotional strength. How balanced are you? What are you doing to make life better for yourself and others? The big-penis fixation is another way human emotions have been commercialized. The more inadequate you feel, the easier it is to commercialize your emotions. If you're insecure, it's easy for corporations to sell you products. When you stop judging yourself, you stop judging others.

Self-love is a natural by-product of the compassion you are evoking in your life. By allowing others grace, you grace yourself.

Risk Management

Every day, I challenge myself to do something that takes me out of my comfort zone. It can be something small, like going food shopping at a new store. It might be something bigger, like travelling to another country on my own. Honestly, there is nothing quite as empowering as facing my fears on a daily basis. Meeting men from dating applications and websites used to be something that added panic to my life, and that is why I undertook it. By pushing myself into extreme situations, I overcame my anxiety of dating.

You probably have your own fears to face. These could be exploring the wilderness, applying for a new job, starting a relationship, or even wearing bright red lipstick! You might have noticed that when I'm on TV, or speaking at an event, I prefer to wear red clothes. I do this on first dates, too. If you are struggling with confidence and emotions, professionally or spiritually, remember to spend time and energy getting to know yourself, accepting yourself, and loving all of yourself. Inner confidence is as important as outer confidence; often, wearing an energy colour or a colour you love can bring you into your best frame of mind.

I challenge myself to do one brave thing every day. I never run out of things, because it usually takes many attempts before I really get over my trepidation. You might find that some things need to be tackled more than once, and sometimes once is enough. Have courage. It gets easier the more you challenge yourself with new adventurous things to do.

Your lifestyle and childhood experiences make you unique. Everyone has different fears to overcome. A lot of unpleasant emotions come from old hurts, other people's baggage, and past negative experiences. Accepting your malaise will help you heal old childhood wounds, even though it can sometimes feel as though you are battling old beliefs that no longer reflect the person you are today.

There are challenges that you can fight and win. So often, people equate self-forgiveness with weakness, or being too easy on themselves. In reality, forgiveness is something that frees you from negativity. Self-forgiveness means taking back your true power. Through my story, I hope to help you be who you are and to understand that you have the power to change your situations.

First, you have to learn to accept and be empathetic to yourself. Then, you learn to apply that empathy to others. When you accept yourself, you accept others. You can release judgement, and consequently the anxiety associated with self-forgiveness.

Release all that that does not belong to you and is not helping you feel sexy.

Fear of Rejection

I am always looking for inspirational people to follow and to "friend" on social media. Sometimes, I come across a person who I connect with, and I have this instinct to follow them on social media and to send a friend request. As you may know by now, I am the woman who meets, greets, and picks up strangers on the road, in coffee shops, on airplanes, and through social networking. You name a way of meeting people in an unusual way, and I most probably have already done it! A friend request to a stranger on Facebook is not out of the ordinary for me. Once, I sent out a friend request to someone I admired; it was rejected, ignored, and deleted. Who knows why? Having a big social media following, I now know that most of the time I miss out on notifications, because I get so many of them. Previously, I did not understand this. My personal well-being improved when I learned to stop making assumptions and inventing stories about the possible reason behind a social media rejection.

At this point, I have to remind you that rejection is never personal. It may feel personal, but it's not. For every no, you will hear ten yeses. The problem is, it's the "no" and the negative connotations that are attached to that "no" that stay in your mind. Always. The human brain loves to ponder negative situations at all times. Every time I face rejection, I remind myself that one person saying "no" does not negate every other good thing in my life. When I started to see things from another point of view, I realized that most rejection is seldom meant as a personal insult. Every time I catch myself feeling a negative emotion from being rejected by someone else, I remind myself that everyone has the right to decide what or who is right for them.

Sometimes, I am the one doing the rejecting!

Releasing Expectations

Why depend on anyone else for your enjoyment? The moment you expect something, you will unquestionably be setting yourself up for failure. Keeping a positive frame of mind, regardless of outcomes, ensures that you will have a good time, whether you are alone or in the company of others. Being open-minded in dating, in parenting, in business, and in everyday life means going with the flow. However, it's healthy to retain certain boundaries regarding the type of person with whom you are interacting.

Inner development is crucial in the quest for self-knowledge; the more you know yourself, the better you can communicate your boundaries with others. You deserve to be selective about how you spend your time. You must spend time with people who are worthy of your attention and emotions. Releasing expectations helps you stay in the now, with the keen ability to assess what is happening. Awareness helps you stay kind to others.

Be Who You Want to Be in Love With

You attract the type of person you are right now. That is true for every area of your life, including work, business, love, and family. You're not the person you were ten years ago at your sister's wedding, or two dress sizes ago, or before having kids. Take a good look in the mirror. You're amazing, just as you are! See the beauty in yourself and accept things as they are right now. Release the expectation of seeing change overnight.

My life is a work in progress; I know yours is, too. Are you approaching life with a lack of enthusiasm, and filled with dread at the thought of facing another lonely day? Do you act surprised when people do not want to stick around when you complain about your ex or put yourself down? If I'm being negative, I know from experience that I'm going to attract more negativity, or worse!

When you're being your sexy self, full of self-knowledge and self-love, authenticity is easier. You will attract your mirrors and kindred souls. That's why you should strive to be genuine.

No one in the world can be a better you than you. Release the need to be perfect as well as the need to be anything other than that which you are, deep in your authentic soul.

Be Selective

You're not going to get along with everyone. This does not say anything negative about who you are. Your own particular brand of magic just does not jive with everyone. They may, in fact, be struggling with their own issues, which makes them treat you in a way that you are not comfortable with. You have the choice to walk away from a person or situation that doesn't feel right.

Some days, you will get turned down. Some days, you must choose to walk away. As you grow in your journey and truly start loving and valuing yourself, someone else's rejection will no longer ruin your life. You will also know how to move forward without hurting someone else's life. You can set boundaries, and you don't need to take on other people's pain and insecurities.

As I get to know myself better, I feel more whole. I feel complete. This awareness of myself has also helped me become more in tune with others. Being so sensitive to auras and energy, I am often able to be more aware of other people and their emotions. I can often see through fake promises, pretentious behaviour, and excuses. I can spot the difference between the genuine and the false as I become more spiritually enlightened and grounded in myself. I attract the same energy into my life. I look for honesty, integrity, and consistency. I am also more aware of how my behaviour impacts others and I strive to be more caring with those around me.

Needing to Fit In

As a part of my Sexy Brilliant journey, I released my need to fit in. I released what the world told me I must be. I encourage you to do the same. Release the labels imposed on you. From now on, every single day of your life will become a masterpiece that you will create out of the flow of the universe and out of your own inner, sexy voice—your intuition.

No more need to sabotage, worry, resist, or drink your pain away. Release it. You are on a journey of self-awareness, leading with love. You have now chosen self-love to guide you in this journey. Your evolution will go on for the rest of your life.

Here are my main suggestions to help anchor your personal changes on a daily basis:

Marry yourself. Self-love will be the most satisfying relationship you will ever encounter. No more need for outside validation. You will feel that pull less and less. No more waiting for needs that remain unmet. No more assumptions and disappointments. It is all about you. Go buy yourself a ring and celebrate the new relationship you have created with the most amazing and sexy person in the world: you. It's time to orgasm and make yourself one with life. You can go to our foundation's website to order your commitment ring. When you have the ring, write your vows to yourself. Say:

> *"To you, my precious one, I will now devote the rest of my life to loving you, purposely, through thick and thin. I will not let you down anymore. I welcome your sexiness without judgement and embrace your brilliance without boundaries."*

Add anything your inner sexy voice tells you to. Create a celebration of love. You can actually say your vows out loud and integrate your new ring and self-loving lifestyle into your journey. To do this, invite people you care about and make your commitment in front of them. This will make you even more accountable to follow through on your vows. Committing in front of other people is a great way to avoid self-sabotage. Make sure that your celebration is of a caliber that expresses the love you have for yourself: keep your standards high. Make this a pivotal day in your life. The best party you ever host should be for yourself. Share pictures of your day with me using the hashtag #imarrymyself. Share your beautiful journey with the world.

Rising Above

It sounds cliché, but finding your purpose in life does start with loving all parts of yourself. Confidence and clarity play a big role in finding yourself. They will lead you to your purpose. People are constantly bombarded with information that they are not good enough, and you might start to believe it. If you do not have time, energy, or emotional strength for your own well-being, you may struggle to increase your confidence. Perhaps, like me, you have gone through your own share of heartbreak, financial loss, or maybe even the death of a loved one. You may have felt completely lost. Through these tough times, you will discover your own strength. Low moments reveal who you are, and your life purpose.

I, too, went looking for answers and eventually found my purpose. This is how I became successful. I started looking!

Let this book be the first step toward the release of the old that does not serve you anymore. I hope some of the tools, tricks, and techniques shared in this book help you in finding your Sexy Brilliant divine calling.

Activity: Chapter Eight

If all releasing was as easy and pleasurable as having an orgasm, the world, overall, would be a lot more open. That is, if you like having orgasms. Not all of us do, and that's okay. If not, I will take the extra orgasms from anyone who prefers to pass. Haha!

Choosing yourself (even if that means you need to be alone) is the first step to releasing. Would you rather drown, but be surrounded by people? Or be reborn, alone?

_____

The ultimate decision you make is neither right nor wrong. Every choice you make either brings you closer to, or further away from, releasing. Yes, it's a tough decision. But making this choice will bring a better you. Remember, you are releasing in order to find your true life purpose.

This is a feat that most people will never face. Are you one of the few ready to live life completely with purpose? What would you do if you knew failure was not an option? What is your ultimate goal? Identifying it will bring you that much closer to true release.

_____

_____

_____

_____

_____

After your goal is identified and even achieved, you are not off the hook! You are here to continue growing and developing. The day you stop evolving is the day you die.

Infinity is what happens when the cycle has just ended. It starts again. And again. And again.

Take a breath. Release.

You will be Sexy Brilliant for infinity. Choose it forever.

Conclusion

End with an Orgasm.

I was sitting quietly, letting go of the thoughts that kept invading my inner peace. With each thought I was doing my best to welcome it with acceptance, contemplate what this moment was trying to teach me, and assume the lesson before releasing it. I did the steps of Ho'oponopono—the Hawaiian practice of reconciliation and forgiveness—and filled my heart with love and gratitude before allowing my mind to once again be at a state of peace. I did this for a while, allowing each distraction to come and go.

Suddenly, my meditation was overpowered by my intense sexual desire. Out of the corner of my eye I saw him in the kitchen washing the dishes. I could not help thinking that his ass looked so good in those jeans. The way the denim faded ever so slightly at the top of his thighs. As he stood there scrubbing the pots, his body rocked ever so slightly and quickly back and forth. He was stirring up all kinds of wild feelings within me.

The light from the window highlighted his silhouette. He seemed calm, relaxed, and lost in thought. As I watched him I couldn't deny that I had an urge to go up behind him and press my body against his. I wanted to feel the warmth of his body and smell the fragrance of his shampoo. I imagined wrapping my arms around him to feel his chest with one hand and let my other hand find its way ever so slowly and gently to the button of his jeans.

What would come next made me hold my breath before I let out a sigh of sheer ecstasy. I thought about him turning around and pulling me into him. His hands still warm from the water. He placed one on the small of my back and the other on my neck as he tilted my head, his lips landing just behind my ear, sending shock waves throughout my body.

He lifted me onto the kitchen table and unbuttoned my blouse...I wanted to f**k him right then and there. Feel him deep inside of me, but at the same time I wanted to savour every moment of his attention. I wanted to let him touch my breasts and flick my nipples with his tongue. I wanted to let him taste me as my desire for him reached new heights. I would not allow myself to cum just yet.

First I would take my turn to test his endurance. Hold his rock hard penis in my hand and feel the throb of desire. I wanted to bring him to the brink of cumming, then make him wait. Then I would tease his penis with my tongue, circling the head a few times before bringing him into my mouth. I loved the power of meeting each other along the way until finally we were both ready to cum together.

At that moment I would invite him into me and together we would ride the wave of ecstasy.

What an amazing fantasy! I took out my toys and lovingly f*cked the shit out of myself until I had cum three times, no guilt, no shame, no more holding back. And I reminded myself there is power in being single.

I started this book with the phrase "Life is an orgasm!"

Too Fat Too Loud Too Ambitious will encourage you to embrace your Sexy Brilliance. You will learn how to be daring. You will scream your truth and put yourself out in the world in a powerful way. You will practice being unapologetic. With this book, you will make your life one of the best orgasms you will ever have.

I decided to end this book with one of my most notorious quotes: "Sometimes I meditate, sometimes I masturbate.

Either way, I find myself."

Your fantasies and life's passions may vary. Your sensitive subjects might not be the same as mine. If nothing else, I hope this book has given you permission to accept and love yourself as you are and to never stop being authentically you. You might fantasize about furries, lace, leather, happy endings, or your life purpose might be saving the rainforest, inventing the next meal in a cup, being the best parent you can be, or you may still be searching for your life purpose.

The scenarios change but the goal is the same. **K**now, **A**ccept, **U**nveil, and **R**elease your beautiful, sexual, creative, intelligent energy into the world as a celebration and acceptance of this life you have been given to experience and explore.

Thank you for being part of this incredible journey.

In love, gratitude, and mutual respect,
Chardi Kalaa,

Devina Kaur

Acknowledgements

Many people have helped me achieve my calling of becoming Sexy Brilliant, and have consequently made this book possible.

Thanks to some of the professionals I have had the good fortune to work with: Marc Dumaine, Sara Gilbert, Ashish Sehgal, Masaki Tomita, Bob, and Dr. Jennie. Gratitude for choosing me as a client.

Book editors, Crystal Jackson, Anneliese Papaurelis, Susan K. Csomor, Suzanne Charlebois, Jade Africa, Alexa Nazzaro, Stephanie Lariviere.

Activity Design, Sabrina Prioletta.

Cover photographer and graphic designer, Suzanne Charlebois.

A big thank-you to the people, friends, dates, partners, neighbours, clients, strangers, and business acquaintances I have had the opportunity to connect with and learn from, who have helped me become a better person. I am thankful to all that you have taught me.

My neighbours, past and present, who are always dropping off food and taking my dogs out for walks.

My firstborn Anahat, for choosing me as a mom and for always making me laugh.

Thank you to my parents for supporting me. I hope you never read this book. LOL.

Final thank-you to you for being here, and for reading my words.

Guru Ang Sang
Devina Kaur

About the Author

Devina Kaur is a creative entrepreneur, researcher, inspirational speaker, host of the Dear Devina radio show, and founder of the Sexy Brilliant™ Global Revolution. She is the creator of The Sexy Brilliant™ Academy of online personal development courses, including: The Power of Being Single, The Heart Break Process, How to Make Money Your New BFF!, and the unique Sexy Brilliant™ Empowerment cards. She has also developed her signature, life-changing K.A.U.R.™ Process, which teaches empowerment through self-knowledge, self-love, and radical self-acceptance.

Devina was named a Top 25 Canadian Immigrant of the Year in 2019 and is the winner of a REX Karamveer Award as a "Champion of Change." Undoubtedly a humanitarian and philanthropist, she has volunteered most recently in India, Rwanda, and Guatemala.

A self-proclaimed accidental author, this full-time single mother is a yogi, a martial artist, and a lover of animals and people alike. Born and raised in a traditional Punjabi family in India, Devina now lives in Montréal, Canada.

Learn more about Devina and her message of empowerment and leadership at www.SexyBrilliant.org.

Made in the USA
Middletown, DE
22 April 2021